A PLACE TO DIG IN

WILLIAM H. HINSON

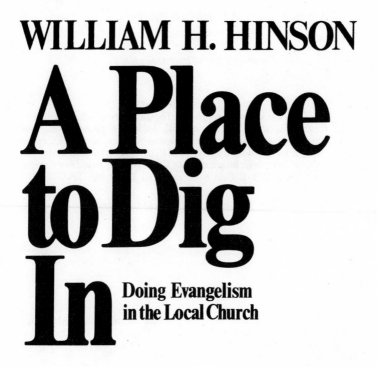

A Place to Dig In

Doing Evangelism in the Local Church

ABINGDON PRESS

NASHVILLE

A PLACE TO DIG IN

Copyright © 1987 by Abingdon Press

ISBN 0-687-31549-2

MANUFACTURED BY THE PARTHENON PRESS AT
NASHVILLE, TENNESSEE, UNITED STATES OF AMERICA

To George Mayo, whose faith, friendship,
and encouragement strengthen me still

INTRODUCTION

Some months ago, before the publication of Bishop Richard Wilke's book, *And Are We Yet Alive?*, the editors at Abingdon Press asked me to write a basic, practical book on doing evangelism in the local church. The wide acceptance and excitement created by the bishop's book increased my own excitement and made me believe that those of us in The United Methodist Church are ready to take seriously the mandate to be evangelists.

The model of evangelism described in these pages has evolved during the last sixteen years of my ministry. During those years, I have been serving churches ranging from 1,200 members to the one I presently serve, which has more than 13,000 members and is located in the center of Houston, Texas. I have been conscious during the writing, however, of my own roots, which can be traced to a twenty-two member church in rural South Georgia. The material within this book can, I believe, be easily adapted to any size congregation.

I had barely begun to write this book when I became aware that the declining mainline churches' greatest need is an entire systems overhaul. Attempts like this book leave many questions begging for an answer. To limit the scope of the discussion has been difficult. Theological discussions were omitted, though any such essay makes one's theological stance obvious. Faithful, effective preaching, the "linchpin" of any church program, was not discussed in any detail. These and many other issues would have easily required additional volumes.

I am aware of at least some of the inadequacies of the book. I am, however, confident of its basic tenets. This model, with some local modification, has been used in a number of different settings and churches, and, in many instances, has met with gratifying success in terms of membership growth. (Two such examples are the Woodlands United Methodist Church and the Airline United Methodist Church in Houston.) I have a personal conviction that when the model is in place and the people are trained, equipped, and inspired, a church will double its active membership every five years. I have seen this happen on more than one occasion.

I am as always indebted to my wife, Jean, for her support, assistance, and understanding. I am also grateful to my secretary, Gail, who not only types my manuscripts, but also helps me find the hours and days necessary to write. I am thankful for my dedicated staff at First United Methodist Church,

Houston, for challenging my ideas, for helping me refine them, and for enriching my own reflections with their convictions. I also appreciate the warm encouragement from the Abingdon editors to finish this book.

CONTENTS

Improve the Climate

When my brother-in-law was a small boy, his parents insisted that he take piano lessons. He was not an avid student and was totally undedicated to the discipline of practice. He did, however, recognize the necessity of playing at least one piece at the annual piano recital, so he memorized one of the simpler pieces of music. He was able to begin the piece when he played it at home by remembering that the middle C on his Wurlitzer piano was right beside the W.

When the day of the big recital came, Miles nervously took his place on the stage and poised his hands in preparation for a dramatic beginning. The silence of the crowd grew ominous, however, while Miles sat paralyzed—his hands fixed and frozen. It seems the people responsible for the recital had provided a Yamaha piano rather than a Wurlitzer, and Miles could not find middle C! After a long,

embarrassing pause, the piano teacher realized what
had occurred, walked onto the stage, put her
embarrassed pupil's hands on middle C, and then he
was able to play his piece. Needless to say, this
episode marked the end of his piano playing career.
His parents gave it up as a waste of money.

Something like the experience of my brother-in-
law seems to have happened to The United
Methodist Church. Once we knew where middle C
was, but the world seems to have traded pianos on us
and we somehow can't get started, can't get things
going as we would like. Our paralysis is showing
itself dramatically in the continuing membership
losses we are experiencing. Our response to those
losses has been marked by confusion and uncer-
tainty, and as of this writing, we are still in great need
of a clear, compelling direction for the work of
evangelism.

At the heart of our confusion is some muddy
thinking about what makes someone Christian. We
have somehow assumed that everyone's spiritual life
is as it ought to be and that it is now the responsibility
of the church to capitalize on the implications of a
right relationship with God. We are, therefore,
spending the capital of previous generations. While
John Wesley spoke to his preachers about having
"nothing to do but save souls," we organize to use
souls. On the one hand, we are appalled at the moral
breakdown within the church among both clergy
and laity, the spiritual erosion among our ranks that
threatens to destroy us—but we, nevertheless,
noisily proceed as though all are securely anchored
in the verities of the faith.

A casual glance at The United Methodist Church's news digest, *Newscope*, and its summary of annual conference actions across the church substantiates the complaint we often hear from some of our laity. The actions of our annual conferences appear to confirm the charge that we have an inordinate amount of social concern and an almost nonexistent concern for the individual spiritual lives of our people. We have engaged the world and are making a diligent effort to call all of its systems and governments to their responsibility in Christ, but are all the while failing to come up with creative ways, means and programs to meet the individual spiritual needs of our people. Consequently, the gaps are growing—the gaps between pulpit and pew, the gaps between boards and agencies and local churches, and the gaps between our episcopal leadership and our people.

Several years ago I met with a large group of persons who were planning specific programs to penetrate our society with Christian claims. We were well into the second day of that meeting before someone, almost as an afterthought, declared, "I suppose we ought to have a prayer." Members of that group certainly recognized that the power of the early church, the power of the church in any age, has never been based purely on economics, nor in the amount of its reserves, but in the church's having been grounded in its relationship to an empowering God. Apart from that relationship, we become just one more ideology jockeying for our position among other secular strategies.

Standing alongside that experience at a meeting with no prayer was a description in a mission magazine of the qualities required of a leader. The article was a good one, clearly and powerfully outlining leadership qualities. There was, however, no mention of God or the necessity of a relationship with the Master. I do not believe for one minute that the persons who outlined the characteristics of leadership and omitted any reference to God really believe that we can be effective as a church through power plays or a refinement of the techniques the world employs for securing change. I believe we have presumed on a repository of values that we have inherited from previous generations. We have forgotten, however, that our own generation needs to know how to handle its own sin, that the requirement of personal regeneration is levied against all people everywhere, and that our ministerial leadership must offer people help and belief for the deep hunger for God that is the necessary prelude to any form of outward service.

None of us would be happy with a narcissistic individualism. It is true that a "born again Christian" without a social conscience is a menace, but the reverse is also true. I agree with Albert Outler, who said that he couldn't be a pietist because they are so selective of their own kind, and he couldn't be an activist because they are so brutal. We Methodists have, happily, traditionally stood somewhere in the middle ground. Faith, for us, must share itself in word and deed. Timothy Simms, writing in *The Christian Century,* December 11, 1985, page 1141, "Learning From the Fundamentalists," had a penetrating question to ask: "As you take your prophetic junkets to the trouble spots of the world, wage war against corporate evil, or work at embellishing your shepherd's staff with the latest pearl of professional development, do you really care whether people around you know and worship Jesus as Lord and God?" I believe that is a question we must continue to raise in the church—especially about every project to which we set our collective hand.

The beginnings of an incorrect assumption could be seen taking shape in the experience of worship, particularly during the 1960s. Worship, in all too many instances, was presented in those days as a pragmatic affair that always resulted in some kind of specific behavior, generally social and public in nature. Our churches became a rallying place, and we were properly grateful for that. But in the process of making worship only a means to an end, personal piety became something of a hoot and we lost the quality Howard Thurman was talking about when he said that Christians should be able to view the world through "quiet eyes."

Somewhere in that frantic activism, when we were meeting at the church only as a springboard for engaging an evil world, we lost our center and began to experience spiritual vertigo. Now, *spiritual formation* has become a buzz word in our denomination. We have long since recognized, however, that we are not purely a populous movement whose positions are arrived at through dialogue and debate, but we, as do all historic expressions of the Christian faith, have a givenness, a faith once and for all delivered to the saints. Our authority does not have to represent anything akin to a cross between Shakespeare, *Psychology Today*, and the *Farmer's Almanac*. The basic spiritual needs of our people have, however, sometimes been neglected because of our preoccupation with the implications of worship rather than the divine-human encounter that is at the heart of worship.

Perhaps, in our search for clarity, we are rediscovering what William Temple meant when he declared that worship is not simply a prelude to service, a means to an end, but is an end in itself. The founders of Harvard put it another way when they declared in that school's charter that Christ is to be "laid in the bottom." He is the foundation of all learning and living. We have, in our eagerness to call the world to Christ, forgotten that all effective ministry is a consequence of Christ's being "laid in the bottom." No one put a higher premium on education and the social expression of the Gospel than John Wesley, but he insisted on the primacy of Christian experience. We mainline Christians cannot give up the correct and necessary tension existing between the personal and the social.

Who is calling our people to a personal relationship with Jesus Christ? Ministers and their people can become spiritually bankrupt, lazy with the luxuries we have inherited, and forgetful of our original vision. Secondhand experiences have always led to second-rate results. We cannot simply dismiss as otherworldly those concerns which were basic for our Lord and for the founder of our denomination. C. S. Lewis has reminded us in a rather dramatic fashion that those persons who have convictions about the next world make the largest contributions in this world. We cannot overreact to the charge of triumphalism to the degree that we become neutralized in our outreach. We may find ourselves in the dilemma Harry Emerson Fosdick spoke of when he declared that in the past the question was, how can we have tolerance when we must live up to our convictions? Now we are concerned with how we can have convictions when we must be true to our tolerance. We must never become so enamored of mutuality, as good as that can be, as to forget that Caiaphas was right: It is necessary for "one man to die for the sins of the people." Our people need more than a peak experience and an expanded consciousness. We need what P. T. Forsyth was talking about when he said that we don't need merely a helper, we need a savior. We cannot enlist our people in the complexities of today's world without, in the same massive effort, grounding them in the verities of the Christian faith.

Admittedly, a pluralistic culture with its accompanying complexities makes the task of evangelism more complicated. I recall standing once at the Vietnam Memorial in Washington, D.C., and watching as grieving families looked for the names of their loved ones. Some of them brought flowers to that black marble monument which bears thousands of names of those who died in the Vietnam war, and some of the mourners came to make rubbings of the names that they might retain them as mementos. I was standing in the middle of that searching, grieving crowd when suddenly a high school choir appeared and began to sing "Let Not Your Hearts Be Troubled, Ye Believe in God, Believe Also in Me." The choir had not finished the first stanza when an attendant rudely interrupted them, saying, "Cut that out! If you sing that here, we'll have to let communists and others demonstrate."

We cannot, however, let pluralism become the guiding force of our ministry. The Gospel must stay at the center and all people must be confronted with its claims and promises or else we are confused at our core.

People are not upset with us these days because of what we believe. People are largely disappointed because they cannot discover what we believe. We do very well in telling people how Christians ought to behave, what they should or should not do, but we rarely give them a word about becoming a Christian. The world can somehow sense that we are off center because we dwell 99 percent of the time on the implications of the Christian faith rather than on the glorious meeting that brings life and changes life.

All across the church the cry I hear from the lay people sounds the same, "We want to be fed." I have heard pastors who have wanted to pull out their hair because of that clamoring demand. I have shared the same kind of impatience with the insistent need of people to "be fed." Oftentimes I have felt like saying to such persons, "Why don't you take the cross off the altar and replace it with a feeding trough? If your only concern is to fill your own spiritual bellies, and if you have no concern for the issues that tear our world apart, why not remove the cross from the altar?" But even as I have grown impatient with their primitive requirement for spiritual food, I have remembered that the first command of the risen Christ to the apostle Peter was that he "feed his sheep," that he "feed the lambs." It is true that although some of our people seem to want to wait forever to take off their bibs and replace them with the apron of Christian service, they can never begin to feed a hungry world until and unless they, themselves, are fed. That is the one requirement that is inescapable for pastors and leaders all across the church. Jim Jones and the horrible experience at Guyana stand as a ghastly monument to the enduring need of people for a basic faith to live by.

During a recent preaching mission in South India, I heard a story from one of the pastors there about an old man who was a Hindu. The old man had lived all of his life in a small village with a polluted well. The people of the village were almost always sick, and no one enjoyed robust health. In time, Christian missionaries came to that village, and as is proper for Christian missionaries, their concern was both personal and social. In addition to the words they spoke about Christ, they dug a well, a good well, for the people of that village. Shortly after the missionaries had left, Hindu government officials came into the village and asked about the influence of the missionaries on the people. They asked the old man, who lived alone in a shanty, if the missionaries had tried to convert him to Christ. The old man responded that they had not. The officials were just about to leave the old man's house when they glanced up on the wall and saw a newspaper picture of Jesus there. Upon seeing the picture, they repeated their question to the old man, "What do you mean they didn't try to convert you? Why do you have the picture of Jesus on your wall?"

The old man explained that he had gone down into the village to buy some fish a few days earlier and the merchant who had sold him the fish had wrapped them in an old newspaper that contained the picture of Jesus. When the old man had seen the picture, he had put it on his wall. The officials raised the question again, Why was the picture there if he wasn't a Christian? Why did he insist on keeping it there? The old man explained, "I had to put it there; it was because of that man that I was given clean water to drink."

People will always raise the standard of Christ in whatever society they live if those who have drunk deeply from the fountain of freedom and forgiveness that flows from his throne continue to offer clean water to people in his name.

We United Methodists, both by heritage and by organization, are uniquely equipped to offer the world clean water in the name of Christ. Not long ago I had the privilege of having dinner with the editor of a large publishing firm. I was excited and challenged by the conversation we had that evening. The editor kept saying in different ways that there is an ever-expanding segment of our population that is calling for a warm religion with substance. More people are responding to simplistic solutions to complex problems. The world is not challenged by a religion that stands at variance with the best thinkers—philosophers and scientists alike. The world will not, as Wallace Hamilton, a great Methodist preacher, has said, "park its brains to save its soul." People want religion with substance, intellectual and emotional. They will not settle for esoteric values, divorced from the warm, caring person of Christ. They want a warm faith with substance. The United Methodist Church was called into being for an hour such as this.

Ted Williams was the last professional baseball player to succeed in batting over .400 for an entire season. It is reported that Williams and his manager, Joe Cronin, had an interesting conversation before the last day of that 1941 season. They were to play a doubleheader with the Philadelphia Athletics, and Cronin offered to let the famous left-handed slugger sit out the games lest he slip below the coveted .400 mark. Ted flatly refused, declaring that if he couldn't hit .400 all the way, he didn't deserve it. The Splendid Splinter would have nothing to do with a batting record that took him out of the batter's box. He played both games that historic day—going 6 for 8 and ending the season with a batting average of .406.

I wouldn't be a part of a church that takes me out of the hurt and the agony of a world in need. I am grateful for a denomination that serves as a headlight for the Christian faith and not as a taillight. Methodist efforts on behalf of equality between the sexes, our witness against apartheid, our stand against war, for instance, will be ultimately applauded by Christians across the world. We must, however, endure some discomfort as a necessary accompaniment to the eradication of sexism, along with racism and many of the other "isms" against which The United Methodist Church has set its face and its being. We can be justifiably proud of our energetic engagement with the real issues that shape our world and the lives of millions. We should, as William Willimon, minister to the University and professor of the practice of Christian ministry at Duke University, suggested, talk more about "what's right with the church."

We cannot forget, however, that the shaping of the world proceeds from the dynamic uniquely offered in Christ. If our efforts do not include him openly and without apology, then we are engaging in self-reformation, employing the techniques of the world, and we fall into the trap of the man who cleansed his house of one demon only to have that one replaced by seven additional ones.

Love for Christ makes it necessary that we identify with his interest in other people. If we love him, we will feed his sheep and do those things which he has commanded. We cannot, however, fall into the trap of offering the gifts and not the supreme Giver. Christianity is not confined to a method through which the quality of people's lives can be raised. As important as raising the level of life is, we have to remember that the way of the world is always insufficient. We cannot achieve all of our Christian goals by employing the techniques of the world. Perhaps the most important truth emerging from our Lord's temptation experience in the Judean desert was his realization that the ends do not justify the means. They never do. Our means and our ends must be centered in the nature of Christ.

We are not universalists. We cannot settle for an unspoken assumption that "everyone's all right," no matter what they believe. The Scriptures will not let us blithely assume that persons of all faiths and persons of no faith will ultimately be warmly welcomed into the Father's house.

We gladly leave to God's prerogative the decision concerning where all persons will spend eternity. We do, however, assume the same bold stance as the Apostles when they declared that "there is none other name given under heaven by which we can be saved." The disciples didn't stutter when they said

"Jesus is the way, the truth, and the life," because the Master himself declared it. There is no magic in death to change that which was lived out in life. God respects our human freedom. If we are not free to be damned, we are not free to be saved. Our attitude toward persons must never begin or end with the unspeakable assumption that the death of Christ was unnecessary, that God somehow blundered by giving his Son when it was not really necessary. We cannot assume that persons have simply, by right of being born, that which was in reality bought by blood on the cross of Calvary. We United Methodists respect the rights of all people, but all people have a common need. We all need a Savior. We must, therefore, testify faithfully and humbly to the saving love of God we have experienced in Jesus Christ.

We have no right to assume Christian behavior from or on the part of persons who have not been introduced to the Savior, nor can we expect, for any length of time, strong financial and political support from people in the doing of Christian concerns unless they themselves are rooted and grounded in Christ himself. To forget that is to abuse our heritage, to empty our churches, and to hopelessly confuse the climate in which the church is called to do evangelism.

Recover Your Confidence

One morning we had a strange visitor to our parsonage. Just as I was going out on the porch to get the paper, I saw something beside my foot that startled me. Only about four inches high, it sat absolutely still. It was a little baby owl, and he would not move. Thinking at first he might be injured, I called for my wife, Jean. She thought he might be thirsty, so she brought him a saucer of water. Still he wouldn't move. We both thought, "We must take care of this little creature."

We went in to call the zoo. No one had gotten up at the zoo yet. We called the humane society, but they weren't in yet either. We kept calling around town to find some expert who might tell us how to respond to the needs of a baby owl. Finally we found a naturalist who said, "Don't do anything to that baby owl. If you will look up, somewhere in a tall tree you will see he is not alone. His mother has told him to sit very still in

order that he might not be seen by a cat or anything
else. It takes about two dark nights for a baby owl to
spread his wings and fly. If you will look up you'll see
his mother."

We went out into the yard and looked up into the
top of an oak tree and there she sat, with those great
large eyes unblinking, fastened on that baby of hers
and everything and anything that came near him.

You and I have learned during the long dark
nights and days of our lives to look up for that one
who neither slumbers nor sleeps, but whose love is
always directed toward his children's good. On a
personal level we have also acknowledged the
ambiguity in our own lives. It didn't take modern
psychology to teach us that; we know we aren't
perfect. We're a mixture. We have acknowledged
who we are apart from Christ, if we've joined the
struggle at all.

Not long ago I went into a car wash in Houston. I
had my automobile cleaned up, bought some
gasoline, went in to pay my bill, and it was sixteen
dollars. I handed the cashier a twenty-dollar bill and
the bill for the sixteen dollars and asked her for a
receipt. She made a mistake. When she handed me
my change, she gave me the receipt and sixteen
dollars in change. I had taken about a half step when
I caught her error. I turned back to her and
explained what she had done. She blushed and
started to thank me for my honesty. Then I did
something I had never done before in my whole life.
It is out of character, I suppose, but I just did it on the
spur of the moment. I said in a quiet voice to her,
"Don't thank me, thank Jesus." She smiled a
knowing smile, and being encouraged by that, I

asked, "Do you know what I mean?" She smiled even more broadly and nodded her head, saying, "I know exactly what you mean."

We can't even be good until we have faced our capacity to be bad, that we are capable of not only the best, but the worst as well. We've learned that about ourselves or else we're either insufferably arrogant or some kind of religious prude that nobody wants to be around. We've come to terms with the fact that we have to look for a savior on a personal level. Like Paul, we can "toil and strive because our hope is set on the living God" (I Tim. 4:10).

That's why we feel a kinship with the Pope when new systems come out in which the Savior is not so prominent. Like the Pope, we are a little bit reluctant to embrace liberation theology so wholeheartedly until it takes at least one additional step. We know it hasn't undergone the rigors of historic discipline, and we also know it doesn't mention the Savior enough. It talks about Mary's song, but not enough about Mary's son to suit many of us. We know that it's good to get people out of "Egypt," and that the theme of freedom and liberation is strong in the Scriptures. We understand that; we know about the Exodus theology. Our forebears did cross the Red Sea, and our feet got wet. We understand that. We know God wants to lift all people, and he wants to deliver us from bondage.

But the basic question for us is, "Out of what bondage into which bondage?" or, "From whom to what or to whom?" We cannot talk about the activity of God apart from his rule. We've had enough, moreover, of self-reformation. Jesus talked to us about the futility of that. He told us that when our houses are all cleaned up and we begin to congratulate ourselves, suddenly seven more demons move in, and then we have eight, and the last state is worse than it was in the beginning. We look for a system with a savior. We look for a method that has a master in it. If he isn't prominent, then we cannot put ultimate trust in it.

I have a young man in my congregation whose father is a missionary in Argentina. Now and again the father comes home on furlough and I talked to him the other day about liberation theology. He said to me, "Well, my big concern is I hear a great deal of talk about Egypt, but not much about Jerusalem."

I suppose this is my biggest problem as well.

Get them out of Egypt to be sure, but go by way of Golgotha. Get all of God's people out of bondage, but carry them by way of Calvary. There isn't any freedom; that's a misnomer. There isn't any such thing as freedom except in bondage to Christ. That's the only source of real freedom there is.

In the airport at Denver there is a corner set aside to display copies of some historic documents. It's called the Shrine of Freedom. There you can see copies of the Declaration of Independence and other important documents in the life of our country. Interestingly enough, there is also in that Shrine of Freedom an instrument of surrender dated September 2, 1945. It's a copy of what the Japanese signed on the day of their surrender. In it they declare themselves willing to issue any order or to take any action as dictated by the Supreme Commander. That's always been true. You cannot erect a shrine of freedom unless it has within it an instrument of surrender. There is no freedom apart from bondage to Jesus Christ. The privilege we have as we call persons to that surrender is a surrender to sacrificial love—the love that redeemed them.

I love the book *Markings,* by Dag Hammarskjold. On Pentecost Day, 1961, he wrote, "I don't know who-or-what put the question, when it was put. I don't even remember answering. But at some moment I did answer yes to Someone—or Something—and from that hour I was certain that existence is meaningful and that, therefore, my life, in self-surrender had a goal." You and I know that that surrender is to Christ; we know his name. His other name is Love, Redemptive Love.

NASA has been a great deal in the news these days, and we're especially conscious of that in Houston. It is one of our largest industries, one of our finest communities. We also have a splendid church in the middle of the NASA community. One of the things NASA has been scrutinizing, of course, is the tremendous cost of exploring outer space. Someone computed that for every pound of moon rock the astronauts brought back to earth, the cost was $400 million. Not even the most wealthy people in the world would want many door stops at that cost, would they?

Yet, when you start to consider what God did on the rock called Calvary, that moon rock is cheap. I mean, an awesome price was paid for us on the cross of Calvary. When we're called to surrender, it becomes the easiest surrender there is because the call is from someone who loved us enough that he laid down his life for us while we were yet sinners. We have learned to put our trust and our hope in him.

When it comes to trusting and putting our hope in Jesus in terms of the problems and complexities of the world, that becomes more difficult. Our problems are so complex. They are so massive, so difficult. We become like the woman at the well at this point. You recall Jesus initiated a conversation with her and after a time he asked her for a drink of water, then turned and offered her living water. She looked about the scene and said, "How can you offer me any water? I don't see any rope. I don't see a bucket and the well is deep." In other words, "You make a claim, but I don't see your ability to follow through and to really pay off."

We're like that. We look at the problems of our world, and we think there isn't any answer. Someone said the other day, "We need to stop looking for answers in our world and start seeking a presence." That's one of those neat little half-truths. Of course we believe in the presence; we have to have that. But just because we don't see any answers doesn't mean God doesn't have an answer. What it does mean is that we are taking our natural limitations, "I don't see any rope and the well is deep," and we are imposing them upon a supernatural God. We're taking the finite and imposing it upon the infinite. Just because we don't see something, we are assuming that this God of ours can only commiserate with us. He can perhaps be the national chairman of the handwringers' society. He can be counted on to be there with us, but he really can't do anything when you come right down to it.

Every year when my church has our confirmation retreat in Houston, we take our boys and girls up to McMahon's Chapel—the first Methodist society established in the state of Texas. The missionaries had to slip over from Louisiana just to hold an illegal meeting on what was a Roman Catholic land. We take them up there to learn something of the history of Littleton Fowler and all those pioneer preachers who made it happen in our part of the world. I go up on Saturday morning and meet them there and then come back on Saturday afternoon. It's a long trip, 180 miles up into East Texas from Houston.

One of our newest members, a young man in the oil business, learned that I was to go up there and back on the same day and he offered to drive me. He said, "I don't want you to have to drive up there and back in the same day and then preach on Sunday. I'll pick you up early in the morning. Don't eat breakfast; we'll eat on the way."

Early the next morning he drove up in his great big Porsche, not one of those cut-off jobs, but a big one, with a sliding roof top and all kinds of paraphernalia. It was the first time I had ridden in a Porsche like that.

The ride was casual, however. We dressed up like Texans with blue jeans. I had on a big Texas belt someone gave me with the outline of the state as a belt buckle. To tell you the truth, it hurts my stomach, but I wear it anyway. It's not very comfortable, but you have to think about your image out there, and you have to wear your boots. Somebody in Georgia gave me a hat before I left, so I looked the part. We got in that Porsche and we started out on our way to East Texas.

We drove for a couple of hours and pulled into a little truck stop to get some breakfast. It had a picture window and when we pulled up into the driveway in front of the picture window, all the natives got the "big eyes." Here were a couple of fellows in a great, huge Porsche, and they waited to see what we were like. We got out and walked inside. It was a smoky little place. Soon they brought us our bacon and eggs and this young layman said, "Pastor, would you pray for our breakfast?" I said, "Sure!" We started to pray, and I'll never forget the look on those folks' faces when I opened my eyes and looked up. Their stereotype had been shattered beyond belief. Here were two cowboys riding in a Porsche, praying in a Texas truck stop. It just blew them away. It absolutely wiped them out. I tell you we need to blow more stereotypes.

One of the ones we need to get rid of is that our God can't do anything. We must tell of a God who spoke and it came to be, who commanded and it stood still. People aren't going for a God who just commiserates with his people, and we can't blame them. They want a God who can move kings and empires. They want a God who is there, but can also act. They want the God revealed in the Scriptures.

Timidity is not a Christian virtue. Paul said, "God didn't give us the spirit of timidity, but of love, power, self-control." Where did we come off with this timidity?

I have a physician friend whose wife is a part of his ministry, and it is a ministry. When he has a patient, especially one on the young side, she always visits that patient for him. Not long ago, she went into a hospital to see a little girl whom he was treating and when she got there she found that the little girl was alone. She was alone because her family was large and very poor. They were so poor that the mother had to stay at home with the rest of the children, and the father couldn't come to sit with his little girl because he was a day laborer.

Here she was, a beautiful little blonde with blue eyes, sitting alone in a hospital room. She had eaten every smidgen of her breakfast. But right there on her tray where the nurse had poured it out of the carton was a great big glass of milk completely untouched. My friend's wife said to the little girl, "Honey, you've eaten all of your breakfast, but don't you like milk?"

The little girl said, "Oh yes, ma'am, I love milk."

"Well then," she inquired, "why haven't you drunk it?"

The little girl responded, saying, "I'm waiting for someone to tell me how far down to drink."

My friend gathered her up in her arms and said, "Drink all of it, honey; it's all yours."

Those apostles said, "Lord, we have left our houses and our families and our boats. We paid an awesome price. What's in it for us?" "Why everything," he said, "I give you the keys to the kingdom. I want you to have it all."

Where does our timidity come from? Why do we wait for someone to tell us how far down to drink? It's all ours. We must go out and claim it. We follow the one who bound the strong man. No one can plunder a strong man's domain until he first binds the strong man. That one has been bound in the life and death and resurrection of Jesus Christ, and now he calls all believers everywhere to come help him plunder the strong man's domain. We have a history. We celebrate a divine event in the past, present, and future. We are not like hamsters on an exercise wheel. We know history goes somewhere. This is not a haphazard universe. This is our Father's world, and we glory in that knowledge; we live in it, and we triumph in it. We put our faith and our hope in that knowledge.

How did John say it? "I wept much that no one was found worthy to open the scroll" (Rev. 5:4 RSV). Then John saw, "a Lamb standing, as though it had been slain" (Rev. 5:6 RSV). He looked at him. It was the lion of the tribe of Judah. He was worthy to unroll the scroll. He can direct the course of human events. So the scroll was brought to that one and heaven resounded with a shout because they realized that all of history, past, present, and future, is in the hands that were pierced on Calvary.

We are God's people, this is God's world, and we can trust him for it. We can trust him in it. Our hope includes a sound eschatology. We don't make a lot of noise about it and we don't get foolish with it, but our hope is secure. That's why we can toil and we can strive. Paul said, "I am sure that he who began a good work in you will bring it to completion at the day of Jesus Christ" (Phil. 1:6 RSV). He is going to bring his work to a conclusion.

Anyone who grew up in Georgia cannot forget how Pierce Harris, long-time pastor of First United Methodist Church in Atlanta, used to talk about our God "striding down the stairway of stars." He used those words when he talked about what God did at Christmastime, bringing us a baby in his arms. Sometimes he used that imagery in another way, saying that God is going to come striding down the stairway of stars with the keys in his hands one day, rattling them, and saying, "It's closing time." We don't take to the streets and shout that and we certainly don't, as some do, try to compute the time and the season or the date. You get in trouble that way. You can sell a lot of books, but you get in trouble.

One author had a bestseller when he said Jesus would return within one generation after the state of Israel was founded. That was in 1948, and the generation would be in 1988; so the time is getting close. *The Christian Century* carried a story about how the author had to recompute that date. He said it really wasn't when the state of Israel was established, that you really have to figure from the time when Jerusalem was united and that was in 1967, so he bought himself 19 more years. He's going to write a book to prove this theory, and it'll be a bestseller. That's all right. We don't argue with these folk. This is the land of the free and the home of the naive, and everybody needs a hobby. If your hobby happens to be going one up on Jesus and knowing something he didn't know and telling the whole world when the second coming is going to be, then help yourself. This is a free country.

We don't do that. We Methodists think that's silly. We've always believed that it didn't matter how high you jump or how loud you shout; it's what you do when you hit the ground that counts. We're tolerant of those folk. We remember what Bishop Arthur Moore said: "Those people will go to heaven too, if they don't run past it."

I don't know if you saw any of the 1986 articles about VE Day, but magazines and papers were full of all kinds of stories about VE Day in Europe. I read one in *Time* magazine that described the horrible conditions in the concentration camps. Between 300 and 400 people were dying every day of starvation, disease, and all kinds of maladies. When the liberators finally came, it was too late for many of the people. One man, lying there, saw the soldiers as they came in to set him free, and he knew he would never live to get home again, not to America. In his dying moments he pulled one of the soldiers close and said to him in a husky whisper, "Would you do this one thing for me?"

The soldier agreed. The man said, "Would you find my wife when you get back to the States and tell her that I had the joy of knowing the war is won?"

You and I cannot be discouraged. We continue to toil and strive because we have the joy of knowing the war is won.

Build and Sustain Leadership

In order to give effective leadership, every pastor needs a core group of dedicated persons who are willing to become praying, studying, working disciples. The size and shape of this group will vary according to the size and needs of the church.

The first group I met with evolved out of a felt need on my part for someone to give understanding and support to my ministry. As we began to meet regularly, I discovered that I was becoming accountable to those lay persons and that my ministry was taking on a new dimension of strength and responsibility. Almost as a byproduct, I soon discovered that our regular meetings were developing leadership qualities among the laity, even as my own abilities were being enhanced, and soon I began to recognize that those with whom I was regularly meeting had become a valuable pool of leadership for the entire church. Subsequently, I have insisted in every church I have served, from a very small church to the large church I presently serve, First United Methodist Church in downtown Houston, that I have at least two small group experiences—one for men and one for women. I believe these core groups are vital for effective ministry.

Perhaps the first question that emerges in the discussion of the formation of small groups is how the group members are found and recruited. Any selection process should give serious consideration to the traditional Christian disciplines. By that I mean the practical disciplines of supporting the community of faith with one's presence and one's gifts should be viewed with real seriousness. Since pastors are looking for persons they can depend upon even in difficult circumstances, we should not be reluctant to investigate a potential member's pattern of stewardship and total involvement in the life of the church. Such barometers are fairly good indicators of basic interests in the church.

We should not, however, be concerned only with knowing who our leaders presently are, but should also be concerned about the development of leaders. My own policy has been, therefore, not to choose this core group immediately upon my arrival at a new parish. There should be a sufficient interval to enable the pastor to observe the response of his or her people to the opportunities for seminars, learning experiences, and so forth. Patterns begin to evolve, and persons who are genuinely seeking to grow and are looking for deeper involvement in their church begin to emerge. Pastors also become more aware of who these potential leaders are through interaction within the congregation and the community. In an intentional search for leadership, the pastor cannot ignore an individual's relationship to the larger community and his or her potential to influence the community for Christ.

The men I am presently meeting with were selected after about six months of observation on my part. The women's group began meeting regularly after about one year. I personally invited twenty-five men to meet with me for one hour and twenty minutes every Thursday morning. (Since the men's group is the older of the two, I will largely confine my discussion to its formation and development. The women's group parallels the men's in almost every regard.) The number twenty-five, while an arbitrary number, is larger than any group with whom I have previously met. Again, the size and needs of the church largely dictated my decision to go with twenty-five. In our mobile society, however, there are generally from three to five persons who are out of the city, sometimes out of the country. Average attendance generally runs about twenty persons.

One of the first questions always raised about this sort of group has to do with the reaction of others to this specific number having been personally invited by the pastor to be in a group that becomes known as "The Pastor's Group." First of all, I believe that we have real precedence for such leadership selection in the person of Jesus himself, who selected twelve to be "with him." Moreover, the group is not "set in concrete" because people are always moving and vacancies are, therefore, constantly occurring. More than that, there are always a few who simply drop out

of the group because they do not find the discipline
to their liking. During the three years this group has
been in existence, we have already formulated two
rolls. We have those who are regular adherents to the
group practices and then there is a larger number of
those who want to be a part of the quarterly
fellowship gatherings we enjoy with our spouses.
Such persons should, of course, be affirmed in their
decision to drop out of the weekly meetings, and we
do our best to relieve them of any guilt feelings for
having done so.

One of the chief reasons why the reaction of the
larger congregation is not unfavorable to my
selection of a small weekly group is the existence of a
larger, mixed Bible study that I lead each Thursday
at noon. When someone wants to meet with the
pastor for a Bible study, that opportunity is
available, together with a lunch, at the church on
Thursdays.

Perhaps one of the major reasons why my men's
group remains relatively small without outside
criticism is that we find it necessary to meet early in
the mornings in order to find a free time for busy
men. Our group agreed upon 7:00 A.M. Some groups,
again depending upon various needs, have met as
early as 6:00 A.M.

Where should the group meet? The answer to that
question can be determined by the availability of
facilities in your community. My first group of men
met in the church because there was no restaurant
nearby. Several of us volunteered to cook the
breakfast, set the table, and to have all things in
readiness when the other group members arrived. I
still remember with fondness how easily each of us

settled into our routine of doing the thing which we did best, whether it was scramble the eggs, fry the bacon, or set the table. The cost of such meals was, of course, extremely low.

Another group in another church met in a private room of a mid-town restaurant, and my present group meets in a country club ideally situated near the center of this city. I believe that a good breakfast is absolutely essential to the success of the group. There will always be those who prefer little or no breakfast, but those who wish to eat heartily should have the option.

In our particular setting, group members may choose a plate of fruit, a bowl of cereal, or may eat more heartily with an omelet, bacon, and such. Always, of course, there is a bountiful supply of juices and coffee. A breakfast that offers variety is the key to keeping individual appetites happy. We do not, of course, order after we arrive. That would waste an inordinate amount of time. Rather, after several weeks, the crew of servers has a pretty good idea about how many folks like what, and they set up the various cereals and fruits on the table, allowing group members to serve themselves buffet-style. Those with heartier appetites receive what has already been prepared in the kitchen. Coffee and fruit juices are always available some 15 minutes before the actual breakfast hour. This gives group members who like to arrive a few minutes early an opportunity to enjoy a cup of coffee and some fellowship before the beginning of the meeting.

While attendance at the meetings is not mandatory, our attendance, nevertheless, is marked by regularity. Each member is assigned the name of another member, and when that person is absent, the other checks to see about the nature of the absence. When someone casually oversleeps, a rare occurrence, other members of the group chide him considerably about the "white ghost" getting him. Anyone who oversleeps finds it much easier to force himself up the next time rather than to endure the good-natured teasing that inevitably goes with such a lapse of discipline.

Attendance is not checked, although an actual roll is taken silently by group members who are present, but all persons are expected to be there unless sick or out of town. Even when a member is out of town, he still pays for his place at the breakfast. The cost of the breakfast, through mutual agreement with the group, is slightly more than the actual expense of the meal. That small amount of overage allows for the accumulation of funds to enable me to purchase books that can be distributed among the members for the enrichment of their own personal libraries.

Since we pay the restaurant for only the number of those who are in attendance, each out-of-town member's payment enables our treasury to accumulate even more quickly. Members of the group are not expected to make their payments weekly. A secretary sends them their bills monthly or quarterly, allowing them to write one check to cover a considerable block of time.

One book we recently purchased with our extra funds was *The Bible in the Wesleyan Tradition.* Because some of the larger churches in Houston have fundamentalists in their pulpits, this inevitably creates a climate in which we must constantly reiterate the Wesleyan position in our interpretation of Scripture. I have found Bishop Stokes's book enormously helpful in the life of our group, and the discussion of that book in conjunction with our Bible study has enriched our exchanges greatly.

Another book that we are currently studying is Richard Foster's *Celebration of Discipline*. Each time we acquire a new book we allow time, sometimes a session or two, for the group members to discuss their insights and to share them with one another. All of this enriches our Bible study immeasurably.

The reader must not assume that we are slavishly committed to Bible study. While I am persuaded that any group will eventually die of its own weight unless there is solid content being fed into it, we do, nevertheless, have the freedom to spend an entire session with someone who is facing serious decisions, problems, and so on.

During the opening weeks of the group's life, each member is furnished a clip-on name tag in order to help each person know the names of the others. The name tags we used are genuine identification aids. A name tag with the person's name typed on it is more of a symbol than a real help. The only *real* name tag is a rather large one with the name, both first and last, printed with a felt pen. We have taught our members to wear those name tags on the right side of their coats. In that way, when a group member shakes hands with another, he or she sees at a glance the name of that person. Normally, after several weeks have passed, the name tags are no longer worn. They are, however, kept available for the group in the event of visitors or new group members. At such times we all wear our identification so that the newest arrivals may know who we are and may learn our names more quickly.

After the breakfast has concluded, we refill our cups with coffee and move to another area of the club where we can be comfortably seated in a circle. We have learned with that transition, that it is not yet an effective time to begin the lesson or the discussion. First of all we inquire about concerns from members of the group. These concerns may take the shape of prayers for family members who face illness, job transition, and so forth, or it may be that the particular day which faces a group member is a crisis in his career. Generally this sharing takes only a few moments because the longer prayer time is reserved for the concluding moments the group is together. This opening inquiry about concerns simply gives an opportunity to "unload" to the member who is carrying a pressing need so he may turn his full attention to the proceedings. We try to make our transition to the circle area and hear those concerns by 7:30-7:35 A.M. Then our lesson begins.

After the lesson and the discussion related to it conclude, we then have a time of prayer. Occasionally I will ask three or four persons to respond to the various prayer requests which have been brought by members of the group. I will, moreover, ask group members to pray specifically for a request. If, for example, three persons have brought a concern to the group, I will ask another group member to pray for one of those concerns, while another prays for another, and so on. We try not to let any single concern go by without a response in prayer.

Prayer time will be varied, moreover, by asking group members simply to pray for the person seated on their right or left. Just a few sentences are called for by way of thanksgiving for the life and friendship and contribution of that particular group member. The intercession almost always includes references to the group member's family and to situations within that family with which every other group member gradually becomes intimately familiar. The following week I may ask group members to pray for the person seated on the other side. This individual intercession for each other and each other's needs has been tremendously helpful and effective in our group. Invariably, I have strong business leaders who say to me that those few words of prayer prayed for them were more than worth all of the effort required to be in attendance at that group meeting. Indeed, there are those who say that they could not make it through the demands of the week without having been undergirded by the support and prayers of their group.

Such exercises in prayer teach group members in an informal, unpressured way how to verbalize concern for each other. Their prayers are simple and straight from the heart. We expect each member of the group to make an attempt at praying. Some of the members do not initially feel free enough to pray publicly. In such cases the pastor or the pastor's substitute simply advises them to say, "I want to add my amen to the prayers that have already been prayed." Before very long, all members have learned that the prayers are genuine expressions of concern such as one close friend would make on behalf of another.

The sharing of concerns and prayer time is always concluded by 8:20 A.M. One of the things group

leaders should be especially aware of is that many
have engagements, and the leader should concur
with the dismissal time decided upon by the group.
In the event someone wishes to talk beyond the
formal ending of the group, that is, of course,
permissible and almost always happens. No one
should, however, be made to feel as though he must
stay beyond the time limit formally established by
the group. Busy people are on a close schedule, and
group leaders must teach members of the group to
keep faith with their time commitments.

Group meetings are not confined to Thursday
morning. Additional activities are planned at least
quarterly. During those quarterly meetings, spouses
are invited and a great deal more time is used by the
group. Frequently, such gatherings occur on an
overnight basis and oftentimes travel is involved.
Emphasis in such meetings is put on a particular
concern or block of material which the group wants
to study, and it is generally constructed so as to have
meaning for the total group, not just those persons
who are in regular attendance on Thursday morning. I have found these quarterly meetings very
beneficial in that they enable group members to
know the circumstances in which each group
member lives. Our prayers for each other can take
more intelligent shape and form when we know each
other's spouses and each other's family situation.

Inevitably, these weekly and quarterly meetings
have spin-offs, in that group members become even
closer by attending sporting events, cultural events,
and other affairs in the community together. In
short, they often become each other's best friends,
not just prayer partners. All such spin-offs and

eventualities, of course, pay great dividends for the Sunday school classes and for the church. The Christian community actually becomes the hub around which these couples' lives are lived.

Now let us give more detailed attention to the content of such core group meetings. The particular group with whom I am presently meeting began by considering Alan Walker's little book, *Life Begins with Christ*. This particular work was chosen because it is an excellent treatment of the biblical understanding of conversion in some of the more prominent New Testament persons. We worked with great care through the various conversion experiences outlined in the book, because I wanted members of the group to be able to verbalize their own experience with Christ or to perhaps reach for a beginning relationship with their Lord. We talked about the dynamics of Christian conversion. We talked about the setting in which conversion occurs, and then in Walker's sequel, *Life Continues with Christ*, we traced the implications of the Christian conversion. I wanted to be sure that members of the group understood that conversion marks the beginning, not the end, of the Christian experience. Both of these discussions generated a great deal of sharing among group members. I encouraged participants to be candid with each other concerning those disciplines which helped them grow, as over against those practices that leave them bored and unmoved.

After establishing some basic understanding about conversion, how it happens and what follows conversion, I then tried to help the group see the implications of Christian experience as it is lived out

within the community of faith. We did that by
studying the Letter to the Ephesians. All gifts are
given for the purpose of building up the community
of faith, and mission is to be understood not in terms
of an elective, but a requirement. These and other
issues were grappled with by the group as we spent
some weeks studying Paul's letter to the Christians
at Ephesus.

Following the study of the Epistle to the Ephesians, we turned to the Gospel according to
Matthew. I follow a certain pattern as I lead these
studies. First, I furnish the group with a notebook
containing the text, with ample space in between
verses to make their notes, observations, additions.
Each group member brings his Bible and his
notebook, as the lesson is not just in the form of a
lecture, but is instead a study and a sharing time.
The group leader should not speak for more than five
or ten minutes at a time without pausing to field
questions from members of the group who have
themselves carefully prepared for the lesson of the
day.

Throughout the biblical studies, emphasis is put
upon the personal sharing of group members.
Group members are rather intolerant of "sermons"
shared by other group members. We state right up
front that we are far more interested in that
individual's observation as the Scripture relates to
him than we are in what someone else "thinks"
about a particular verse. Group members want to
know how the scripture relates to them as they
interact with the world. They are not interested in
an ethereal concept that has no meaning, help, or
direction for them.

The group leader must, of course, do careful exegesis on all of the biblical passages. He cannot, however, have an effective Bible study by spending the first half dozen sessions on things like historical background. The interest of lay people can only be kept by those leaders who are able to plunge right into the study in a verse-by-verse exposition, carefully adding related historical details as the study calls for them. Those leaders who have tried the seminary model of Bible study have discovered that their group will not remain attentive. Pastors must learn how to teach, using a method and an approach different from the one most of us were exposed to in seminary.

The skillful group leader will have immersed himself in all data related to a text interpretation. However, lay people cannot be expected to stay vitally interested in such a presentation over a number of weeks. The skillful teacher will learn how to insert valuable background material in the study that will increase group interest rather than decrease it.

Lay people, for instance, are not stirred by the conversation concerning the authenticity of the story of Jesus' dealing with the woman taken in adultery. Many academic questions can, or course, be asked about that text. Lay people are interested, however, in the basic question—does it tell us the truth about the character of Jesus and his dealings with persons who have sinned? If it is true, how does one appropriate that truth in one's own experience and world?

Learning how to be an effective teacher of the Scriptures is one of the great needs of our church in this current day. We have ample courses on preaching, but we do not have courses on teaching. Our people are desperately hungry for solid material supported by careful, but practical, scholarship. In our failure to provide such teaching, we are driving our people to a study of the Scripture that is not always scholarly in its approach and is oftentimes self-centered and misleading in its application.

During our sessions together, I challenge members of the group to personal growth and commitment. I will, for instance, ask group members in a very straightforward way what is the most difficult thing for them to bring under the Lordship of Jesus Christ. I will ask them to share their greatest difficulty in prayer. I will inquire about the hold that money may have on individual lives and the resulting inability to share. Not only do I challenge members of the group as our closeness grows, but members of the group begin to challenge each other. They also feel the freedom to challenge me, and that is extremely valuable for my own personal growth.

I have found it most beneficial to lead my group from a position of weakness rather than one of strength. They know I do not have all things together, and they are intimately acquainted with the various struggles in my life. I also share some victories with them so that the group does not become a giant Band-Aid to patch up the preacher's wounds. (You know the group is growing when joys are shared easily.) In all of my sharing, I endeavor to be honest with them, honest enough so that they can be honest with me. My honesty not only helps them feel free to share their struggles with me and with each other, but it also enables me to be honest with myself. My ministry has always been assisted by at least fifteen or twenty people in my congregation who have been unafraid to tell me when they thought I was kidding myself or posturing for the sake of others. We preachers need someone who will tell us the truth. The truth telling I experience from my close personal friends in my Bible study groups is a line of accountability without which the strength of my ministry would suffer enormously. I have found my Bible study groups quite adept at keeping the preacher from "blowing smoke."

What are the other pay-offs for meetings of this kind? The results are too numerous and too spectacular even to identify them all. Perhaps the first result is an improvement in the pastor's preaching ability. The closeness that results when the pastor and lay people study together grows and becomes a veritable gold mine of homiletical materials. By homiletical materials I am not, of course, speaking of intimate sharing or personal illustrations that would identify or embarrass group members. I am speaking of the identification of human needs within the congregation. If preaching is "giving God's answer on Sunday to the questions people have been asking all week," then a group of the kind I have been describing is enormously beneficial to the preacher. Such interaction always keeps the preacher on target and saves us from the peripheral and the nonessential.

One of the greatest contributions an astute group of men or women can make to their church is to help the chief administrator—the pastor—evaluate various programs and ministries. Every pastor is made smarter by the candid observations and insights of a

supportive, challenging group. Pastors must trea-
sure such sharing and show themselves flexible
enough to make changes, sometimes dramatic ones,
and to shift direction. The Apostle Paul, a Jew, was
"under obligation both to Greeks and to barbarians,
both to the wise and to the foolish" (Rom. 1:14 RSV).
Apparently Paul learned from everyone. Such
willingness to learn from others is the stuff of which
effective leadership is made.

The ensuing strength that inevitably comes to
those who take the study of the Scripture seriously
and who engage in the discipline of prayer,
especially intercessory prayer, makes an enormous
impact upon the total community of faith. Even in a
church the size of First Church, Houston, the
growing spiritual strength of my Bible study groups
has made an enormous impact upon our congregational life. Members of my core groups become the
task forces on whom anyone can completely
depend.

When, for instance, we faced the tremendous task
of underwriting the cost of a block of downtown
property, it was members of my core group who
spearheaded the effort. They literally worked day
and night on the telephones, leading volunteers in
contacting every resident member within our
13,000-member congregation. They did it, moreover, within the span of two weeks. They formed
committees who got out mailings, stuffed letters,
and so on. Not only did they do all of the leg work, but
they also led the congregation in the amount of their
giving. They were the persons who gave five-minute
testimonies from the pulpit urging the congregation
to become involved in the effort to procure the land.

They led an all-night prayer vigil before pledges were made.

They have also been the leaders in raising the annual church budget. Their leadership has been the prominent force behind the 100-percent plus increase we have experienced in our giving over the last three years. Their strong voices on the Administrative Board, the Committee on Finance, and in other leadership positions have been largely responsible for increasing the amount of our benevolent giving. In short, this group gives to a pastor approximately forty persons upon whom he or she can place explicit faith. Wherever there is need in the community of faith, members of the core group can move in with their leadership and skills and make a difference. The difference they make is made primarily because of their commitment, a commitment that is being strengthened and supported in a regular, systematic fashion.

The core group becomes for me an ever-growing pool of leadership from which the local church can draw its leaders. Growing committed Christians who engage in the classic disciplines of our faith can, over a number of years, make a dramatic difference in the life of any congregation. These persons know the mind and heart of their pastor, and their pastor knows their strengths and weaknesses. We can complement each other beautifully. I cannot envision putting anyone into a crucial place of leadership in the local church until there is some commonality established through an exchange of thoughts, prayers, and disciplines.

Not only has our group made a dramatic difference in the amount of our church budget, but they

have also shown themselves to be effective evangelists. Given an adequate understanding of the
Scriptures, Christians come to realize that their
baptism is also their ordination and that they are
called to be multiplying members of the body of
Christ. Core group members are especially sensitive
about reaching out with Christian concern to the
people about them. Such reaching out results in a
constant stream of visitors brought by this group,
sharing in the Sunday school and the worship life of
the community.

This group must, in my opinion, form the nucleus
for organizing to "do evangelism" in the local
church. We cannot depend upon undisciplined,
untrained, unmotivated, ill-equipped persons to be
regular and systematic in their service to the church
of Christ. We must find our leaders, train them,
equip them, and support them on a regular and
continuing basis.

Any discussion concerning core groups and the
life of the local church cannot conclude without an
additional word about finding the time for leading
such meetings. Whenever I issue a challenge to
pastors to begin such groups, I am always confronted by the old problem of people not having time
to do such things. In my experience as a pastor, I
have discovered that I do not have the time to *neglect*
such meetings. I desperately need the support, the
strength, and the insight which such gatherings
bring, not to mention the leadership the members
eventually provide for the entire church.

For the last several years, I have been teaching
three Bible studies. The first group, the one I have
been describing above, meets early in the morning

and is comprised of men only. The second Bible study is at noon and is an open meeting involving men and women, many of whom I do not know. The group has over one hundred in attendance and they come from the downtown office buildings that surround our church. They meet for a lunch provided by the church at a nominal cost and for a thirty-minute Bible study that I lead by lecturing. The third group meets at 1:30 in the afternoon and is comprised of women. These, too, have been invited by me, and they follow the same format as the men with the exception of breakfast. Coffee is substituted, thereby giving us more time to study than the men have. Many of these women are spouses of the men in the early group, but not all of them. A nursery is, of course, provided for those who have small children.

For a number of years, I have made it a practice to spend the first four hours of the day in my study at home. The study is located behind the garage, apart from the house, and with a telephone that does not ring. I have steadily refused to accept invitations for early morning speaking engagements. The only time I break this rule is when I am out of town on a preaching mission and on Thursday mornings when I meet with my core group. When I meet with the men on Thursday morning, I am almost one hour late in getting to my study. That hour I lose on Thursday mornings, however, can be compensated for by getting to the study earlier on Saturday afternoon.

I have discovered that people are able and anxious to meet for something that is helpful and meaningful for their lives. The group with which I am currently

meeting is the latest morning group I have ever
had—they meet at 7:00 A.M. Lay people can meet
with their pastor if the pastor is willing to get up early
enough to accommodate their needs. If you continue
to push the clock back, sooner or later you will find a
time when there is no conflict for any of those men
who wish to meet with you.

All of the groups study the same subject. While we
may be at different places in the study, we
nevertheless have the same content, because
sermon preparation and writing requirements would
not permit me to do preparation for three separate
studies, with different materials. Each group proceeds at its own rate of study, but all of us are
proceeding over the same materials.

I encourage pastors who do not feel that they have
the time or energy to begin such groups to try them
diligently for a period of six months. I believe that
you will find, as I have, that such group interaction is
so important that it quickly becomes one of the most
important aspects of one's ministry. Such meetings
can quickly become the high point of a pastor's
week. Members of my group know that when I am
not there, I have an absolutely irreconcilable
conflict—that it is impossible for me to be there.
During such absences, I have an associate who leads
the group or any member of the group can lead the
session. That is not a big problem for us, however,
because I am rarely absent.

Group interaction can be very threatening to a
pastor. It is sometimes tempting for those of us in
ministry to avoid those situations that call for more
than strong affirmations. Ministers can hide in
studies, spend untold hours on church bulletins,

newsletters, and such, or they can open themselves to a growing relationship with fellow strugglers. I have found lay people eager to be with their pastor in an informal, learning, sharing situation. They do, in fact, seem to learn a great deal more from my shared struggles than from my carefully worded pronouncements.

Be a Leader

In Edward Gibbon's classic, *The Decline and Fall of the Roman Empire*, his famous chapter on the causes of the rapid spread of Christianity is quite insightful. He describes the growth of a faith in an environment that was very hostile to it. There was in that growth a development, which he could not deny, though he himself was unsympathetic toward it. That development, which he assigned first place in the list of causes for the spread of Christianity, was that all new converts considered as their sacred duty the distribution among their friends and relatives the inestimable blessing which they had received (Elton Trueblood, *Your Other Vocation*, page 48). Pastors cannot, however, make it the most sacred duty of their members to impart among their friends and relatives the inestimable blessings which they have received unless it is also their most sacred duty. The pastor must be deliberate and altogether intentional in his or her commitment to evangelism in order to correct the downward drift in the denomination's membership.

Our Lord gave us many clues as to the nature of his calling and the reasons for his ministry. He was never more succinct, never more clear, however, than when he described his mission, saying, "For the son of man came to seek and to save the lost" (Luke 19:10 RSV). We may quibble for years about the meaning of "lost." If we begin to believe, however, that "salvation can come to our houses" in the historic fullness of the meaning of salvation through any other system or means than by our Savior, then we will have lost our evangelistic fire. Richard Niebuhr spoke with derision about a Gospel that can speak of "a God without wrath who brought men without sin into a kingdom without judgment through the ministrations of a Christ without a cross" (*Theology in the Wesleyan Spirit*, Albert Outler, page 60). Jesus said he came that "we might not perish." If there had been any other way to save a lost and dying world other than through the sacrifice of his son, God would have been a monster to have sent him.

Richard Baxter has reminded us that "men will never cast away their dearest treasures upon the drowsy request of someone who does not even seem to mean what he says" (*Leadership*, Fall 1985, page 16). People do clutch their treasures tightly, especially the gift of time. We cannot motivate busy, distracted people to join us in the work of evangelism if our own commitments resemble Swiss cheese. Our crippling mental reservations about the necessity of an encounter with Christ as Savior and Lord have become painfully apparent to those who hear us preach and teach. We must believe in the necessity of evangelism—bringing people to Christ through word and deed—before we can be effective in doing the work of an evangelist.

We have been severely hampered in fulfilling our responsibilities as leaders in the work of evangelism because our seminary training was, for the most part, designed to teach us how to keep the institution we were inheriting intact. Our responsibility was essentially in terms of maintainers of the institution.

We now have an entire generation of preachers who have never experienced growth in membership in the church and who are constantly meeting to bemoan membership loss, but are unable to come up with any kind of plan to reverse the situation, even on their own local level. Some are sounding as though they resent having inherited a church with a dwindling membership.

Far from being aggressive leaders who are unafraid to pioneer a new and creative movement, we are mostly reactive in our personal dealings with those who come to us looking for help. One recent seminary graduate amused a group by saying, "When someone comes to me saying he wants to become a Christian and asks how he can do that, I say to that person, 'I hear you saying you want to become a Christian.' "

There is among us a kind of awkward embarrassment that leaves us free to talk about the need for evangelism, but practically paralyzes us when it comes to doing the work of an evangelist. Can Christ set a person free from sin? Is sin still a reality in our

culture? Even if we cannot as individuals get a
handle on some of the systemic evil in our time, can't
we at least furnish some clues as to how we can
handle our individual guilt? Shouldn't a pastor be
adequately trained in evangelism to the point of
being able to quietly kneel with a searcher and lead
such a one in the making of a verbal commitment to
Christ?

I am not suggesting a type of evangelism that
resembles the Elmer Gantry motif, nor a crass
manipulation, nor a simplistic approach that takes a
few answers and imposes them on an entire
population. I am talking about the necessity on the
part of every minister of knowing what to say or do,
when someone asks, "How can I become a
Christian?" We must know how to respond to such a
request, not only in terms of what a Christian does,
but who a Christian is. We must take the lead in
helping people to see Christ as he is and to see
themselves as he wants us all to become.

There are no shortcuts to true leadership. Pastors
who have water and a towel as a symbol of service
must constantly be on the guard against substituting
words for actions. Bernard of Clairvaux had it right
when he said that if you would do the work of a
prophet (or an evangelist), you will not need a
scepter but a hoe. To be a leader in any area requires
a substantial allotment of time to the particular
endeavor in question.

Pastors would do well to keep a diary in order to
check themselves on how much time is actually
spent on prospect contact and cultivation. We are
sometimes shocked by the realization that several
weeks have gone by before we follow up on a lead or

continue cultivating a new friendship. We find it much easier to talk about evangelism and to settle for a vague desire to make the church grow than to give large blocks of time to smart, well-planned programs and actions. Workshops and rallies certainly have their place in terms of instruction and motivation for evangelism. They cannot, however, be a substitute for the doing of evangelism. The church will begin to grow as pastors individually pick up the responsibilities of cultivation, follow-up, and witness.

Recently I asked a group of pastors in a distant city to keep an honest journal on how much actual time they gave to doing evangelism. They were pastors of growing churches and were considered very aggressive leaders. They were shocked when they realized that not one of them had spent more than four hours per week doing the most important work in the life of the church—the work of evangelism. We must constantly check ourselves to prevent self-deception, from replacing actual labor with words. Thinking, reading, talking, and rallying about the work of evangelism can never replace the necessity of our being evangelists.

As shepherds, we must recover our passion for the lost sheep. At First Church, Houston, our members move frequently. We transfer persons to every corner of America. Some of the stories they tell us, as we try to stay in touch with them, are distressing. We always encourage them to find a new church home shortly after their move.

They attend their new church, however, sometimes for more than eight or ten consecutive Sundays without so much as a telephone call or a post card from any person on the staff or in the church membership. They resist, moreover, having me or any other member of the staff prod the pastor of the church where they are visiting. They maintain that unless the pastor responds to their weekly registration or attendance and the careful completion of a visitor's card, they do not want to be members. They don't want to be contacted just because a former pastor insisted that they be visited or called. One family told me that after two months of regular visiting at a United Methodist church in their new city without any kind of response, they actually handed a written note to the minister requesting a telephone call in order that they might transfer to his church.

A couple of weeks later they called to tell me that they still had not received a response, but this mature couple, deeply devoted to The United Methodist Church, maintained that they were going to join "if they had to knock down the doors to get in."

Such indifference to requests for admission to our churches is admittedly rare. Insensitivity to the needs of the people, however, is unfortunately not so rare. We have discovered that having a hot line in our conferences, or even across the country, is not the only answer. Somehow those who have taken a vow to go from door to door are now having a difficult time "letting their fingers do the walking."

It isn't enough simply to identify the prospects and let them go unvisited. We must cultivate a passion that issues in a concern for the strength and well-being of the total community and all of its people. What has become of the passion reflected in the words of George Whitefield, the warm-hearted preacher who was a contemporary of John Wesley?

He said that "I will go to prison for you and I will go to
death with you, but I won't go to heaven without
you." United Methodist people will get excited about
evangelism when they see the passion of the good
shepherd himself reflected in the faces and lives of
their pastors.

How does one get to be a leader anyway? Authority
means the right and power to command, to
determine or to lead. Even the enemies of Jesus
recognized that he spoke with authority. When
ministers are ordained, they are given authority to
preach the word and to administer the sacraments.
Along with that authorization comes, of course, the
authority to lead the congregation. How one moves
from ostensible authority, that is the recognition of
one's ministerial credentials by the organized
church, to the actualization of that leadership in the
congregation is something all of us should consider.
We have always had the dual task not only of verbally
speaking God's word, but also of expressing it in the
way we live our lives.

The Winter 1985 issue of *Quarterly Review* (Vol.
5, No. 4) contains an interesting discussion on the
source of pastoral authority and authenticity,
according to the *Thinking of Kierkegaard* by Barry
L. Snowden. Kierkegaard's thoughts, combined
with the typology of pastoral authority developed by
Jackson Carroll at Candler School of Theology at
Emory University in Atlanta, remind us of the
dangers of the institutionalization of authority.
Authority based entirely on a minister's credentials
is certainly a far cry from the authenticity
emanating from a minister's personal struggle for
sanctity.

One's authority to lead must be derived not just from the recognition of one's credentials by the church, but also from one's day-to-day living out of the faith. If the ring of authenticity is not heard in the preaching and leadership of the pastor, then a contradiction between word and deed without a corresponding confession and recommitment to an imitation of Christ destroys the credibility of our leadership. Kierkegaard declares that the validity of the proclamation of the word from the pulpit and the administration of the sacraments at the altar rests squarely upon the personal sanctity of the pastor.

One of the nagging concerns I have heard about as I have traversed the nation in speaking engagements is the unenthusiastic worship patterns established in many of our United Methodist seminaries. Admittedly, I have not visited all of them or even a majority of them. I have, however, had the privilege of slipping into chapel worship in several seminaries and have been appalled to see only a few scattered worshipers. My concern stems from the knowledge that there are at least several hundred students enrolled in the schools of theology, and a handful in attendance at chapel is not a good statement about the centrality of worship. Such carelessness in worship can be explained, of course, by class conflicts, student appointments, library visits, and so forth, but we must never lose sight of the fact that ordination does not automatically make us worship leaders if we have not cultivated the art of worship within ourselves. What does it do to our integrity when, upon our first assignment as a pastor, we begin to insist that the laity engage in regular, disciplined worship when we have not taken advantage of the opportunities of worship in our student life? The laity pick up on the variance between the authority that comes from an authentic life and that which emanates from a framed paper on the wall.

The pastor's entire ministry is constantly undergoing evaluation by his or her people. This is especially true when the pastor is endeavoring to be aggressive and forward-looking in terms of ministry. Mature laity do not, of course, require perfection of their pastors, but where there is a gap between pronouncements and performance that is obvious (even when it is on a largely practical level), the ensuing loss is always reflected in an inability to lead the congregation.

Recently I visited a church in another state that was experiencing severe financial problems. In an attempt to shore up the treasury and to pay some of their bills, the pastor had issued a dramatic challenge to the congregation to double up on their giving over a period of several weeks in order to help the church catch up on its financial obligations. Many of the members responded to the challenge, including persons who were on fixed incomes and were already living on a subsistence level. It was devastating to that pastor and to his ability to lead when, in the weeks that followed the special campaign, the word leaked out through an unprofessional financial secretary that although many had increased their giving during this special campaign, some sacrificially so, the pastor had not increased his.

The penalty levied against this pastor was probably more severe than was merited. One cannot, however, preach on tithing and sacrificial giving and expect the church to respond unless one takes the leadership and becomes a sacrificial giver. Experienced pastors know that while such concerns may seem to be largely mundane and altogether practical, they are the very stuff of which leadership is made. I have not ever served as the pastor of a church, including the one which I presently serve, where the leadership was not challenged by the giving pattern of the pastor. We cannot simply make pronouncements about the basic disciplines and requirements of the faith just because it is "our job" and our right as ordained persons. Such pronouncements remain empty and lacking in power. We can lead and move the church forward when we are making an honest attempt to close the gap between words and deeds in our own lives.

Incarnational ministry has always been the most effective expression of Christ. People always respond more to who we are rather than to what we say. Paul in his epistles to his spiritual son, Timothy, insisted that he was to "set the believers an example in speech and conduct, in love, in faith, in purity." Setting the believers an example and "living a life worthy of the Gospel" has always been an awesome responsibility, but we must assume the burden of representative ministry. The Council on Bishops recently stated that the erosion of holiness within the representative ministry is one of the greatest issues threatening our church today.

No one eagerly embraces the burden of expectation that is placed squarely upon the shoulder of one who would incarnate the Gospel. I can still recall the difference between my reception in a smalltown barber shop in South Georgia, when I had newly arrived on the scene as an unknown pastor, and the way they received me after I had been there for a number of months.

In the beginning, before I had had the invocation at the PTA or given the devotional at the Lions Club, and no one knew I was a pastor, I was just one of the boys. I watched with some small interest the childish games of chance played around the soft drink machine as they drew bottles to see who won the pot by drawing the bottle that had been made farthest away. I heard the smutty stories and listened to some of the gossip of what was going on around town.

Then, as soon as my identity was known and the word had gotten around that I was a pastor, the barber in the front chair became the sentinel. Each time I walked in the door he spoke in overly loud tones, "Good morning, Preachurr!!" With the announcement of my arrival, all the usual activity ceased, and the crowd which had congregated in the back sat around in cherubic fashion, waiting until the representative of the church was gone. I resented that childish game of hide-and-seek with the preacher and still do.

Nevertheless, I have begun to accept the weight of the responsibility that comes with the belief that the presence of a pastor is supposed to make a difference. If it does not, then we are no longer the salt of the earth or the light of the world, and it isn't any wonder that the bland are leading the bland into every ditch in sight and mediocrity is the order of the day.

Those of us who are in the representative ministry have always had to struggle with the temptation to

be "one of the boys" or "one of the girls." When we
are swallowed up as having essentially the same
norms, the same values, then the spotlight is taken
off of us and the burden of expectation decreases
greatly. We may be seeing some attempt to
legitimize giving ourselves some relief from the
weight of the burden of personal example in
representative ministry by making so much of the
dichotomy between personal time and professional
time in the ministry.

While all of us recognize the necessity for
withdrawal in order to reengage the world, for the
establishment of a meaningful rhythm in our
Christian life and ministry, we have nonetheless
seen a new emphasis upon the delineation of a
dichotomy between who we are when we're "on
duty" as over against who we are when we're "off
duty." God has not called us to be a stuffed shirt
pietist who makes arrogant claims for ourselves, but
neither has he called us to be one person publicly
and another person privately. We cannot turn the
ministry off and on as with a faucet. Our integrity as
ministers is at stake and that requires us to work
toward genuine wholeness and holiness in life.

The Greeks keep on coming, just as they came to
the disciples with the request to see Jesus. They
keep coming because of an inordinate hunger and a
driving desire for personal regeneration. One of our
basic responsibilities as representative ministers is
to live a life through which God can make his appeal.
We may shrink from the thought of being an
incarnation of the Gospel, but unless our people see
that we are committed to and stretching toward such
an incarnation, we will never effectively lead them in

any endeavor. A vague dispensation such as being "the preacher in charge" is good enough to afford one a parsonage and a minimum wage, but will never galvanize the people into strenuous, demanding ministry for the cause of Christ. Doing the work of a leader requires us to be leaders.

Several months ago I was invited to preach in a suburban church here in Houston. I was startled as I walked toward the pulpit to see a fire extinguisher attached to the side of the pulpit. It was the only fire extinguisher visible to me. At first I thought such a site selection strange. Upon reflection, however, I believe the fire extinguisher was carefully placed. If and when a great fire begins to burn in our churches, it will have begun in the pulpits. If it does not start there, the people in the pews will never have their own hearts set ablaze.

Set the Stage for Growth

People do not grow without a challenge. Busy, distracted persons must be asked from the authority of the Scripture, in no uncertain terms, to redirect their lives and to set new priorities. The preachers who issue the challenge must be very clear about the directions and must not have the challenge emptied of its power by overtones of doubt and vagueness. We cannot enlist the laity in the cause of evangelism, or any other cause, until our invitation to them rings with compelling clarity and until we are properly prepared to guide their response and to direct their enthusiasm.

One of the difficulties we face in the mobilization of our people is the malaise into which they have been driven by repeated challenges with no follow-through. They have responded on a number of occasions but were left feeling like a horse that had been led to water but was not permitted to drink.

Pastors do not have the right, morally or otherwise, to challenge people to engage in ministry unless they are prepared to train and enable those who do respond to fulfill their calling. It is unethical to rant and rave about every Christian's baptism constituting an ordination event if one simply makes the point and leaves it there.

The future of the church is with the *laos*—the people of God. That's where it has always been. The repository of faith does not reside in the seminaries, the boards and agencies, or the clergy. It resides where members of the covenant community live out their faith and appropriate their commitment to Christ through obedience in the world. Our people are eager to respond when properly challenged, trained, and equipped. They alone have the strength and numbers to revitalize our denomination.

The strong financial support they are still providing is a testimony to their strong loyalty. While they do not identify with the news magazines and newspapers' designation of United Methodists as members of a "liberal" denomination, they nonetheless continue to believe in their heritage as those whose inner holiness should manifest itself in outer service.

Millions of our peripheral members have long since left our denomination. The leanness of our church rolls sets the stage for a great leap forward in the field of evangelism. The people are more ready to accept the challenge than their leaders are to issue it.

The church must position itself for growth. Recently, First Church, Houston elected to purchase a block of property in downtown Houston. The property is located diagonally across Main Street from our current facility. In preaching to our people about the necessity of acquiring additional property for future parking needs and expansion, I told them we were positioning ourselves for the Twenty-first Century. Church growth people have made the point abundantly clear concerning the necessity for parking, buildings, and such, that lend themselves to growth. It is not my purpose to review all the factors that prepare a church for numerical growth. My intention is to speak of setting the stage within the group life of the congregation.

Before a church can grow, the stage must be set by making that congregation a functioning center of Christian nurture and mission. There is no time line concerning the readiness of a church to grow and its ability to start growing. One does not need to wait until the temperature has risen in order to start the process of growth in one's church. The stage can be set, and the church can begin its outreach simultaneously. Effective growth and assimilation cannot occur, however, until a church takes on those qualities that are immediately obvious to anyone who shares in a learning, worshiping experience with the congregation. A church is ready to grow and to preserve its membership when even a casual visitor comes through its doors and remarks to another that he or she could tell the difference in that church simply by coming inside its walls.

People in our denomination represent a great reservoir of varied talents and abilities. Even the smallest church has persons within it who can make a real contribution to congregational life. We must use those talents in at least several basic areas in order to set the stage for church growth. We must

take care of our people through congregational
care—hospital visits, nursing home visits, the
visitation of homebound members, grief calls. No
matter what the ratio is between ministerial leadership and membership of the church, no pastor is able
to meet all the needs of his or her people. The only
really effective ministry is that which results when
people are in ministry to and with each other on a
one-to-one relationship.

Robert Scott, the explorer, made a perilous
journey to the South Pole, but you will recall he died
on his attempted return. On the last page of his
journal there is a penciled-in entry, the last entry he
made in his journal. It was really in the form of a plea
directed to the English people. Robert Scott pled,
"For God's sake, look after our people" (*Sunday
Evening Sermons*, Harper & Brothers, 1952, page
162).

People will not join a church or stay long within a
community that does not resemble the body of Christ
in its caring concern. Our people have sensitivity to
that need, and in many of our churches there is
genuine caring on the part of Christians without any
benefit of clergy leadership, training, or direction.

How much more effective it is, however, when
there is organization and people are given an
opportunity to make a definite commitment to the
congregational care ministry and are properly
equipped to do it. When I say a "definite commitment," I am speaking of an opportunity to sign up,
perhaps at the conclusion of a service of worship,
and to become a part of a group of people who are
specifically committed for one or two years to the
ministry of congregational care.

Persons who are enlisted for this ministry should be told at the time they are challenged what the nature of the invitation includes. They should be required to attend a number of training sessions by a qualified leader, and they should be told how many visits they are expected to make and for how long they are to serve. They should be given proper recognition and should be honored both when they accept the challenge and again when they complete their term of service. In our church, we invite our people to make a public commitment by bringing their cards forward and handing them to the minister of congregational care.

I have discovered that many Methodist people are eager to make a public declaration of their faith. This declaration is not pharisaical in nature, nor is it a desire simply to be a religious show-off. It is a recognition of the fact that one commitment alone does not last a lifetime. People are in need of renewing their commitments. Pastors are faced with the ever-present challenge of finding creative ways to call their people to a commitment in which they bring more of themselves under the Lordship of Christ. We must not assume that just because a commitment has been made, it is sufficient for a lifetime. We are those who are saved and are being saved.

The Sunday school is the most effective "port of entry," according to church consultant Lyle Schaller, and place of assimilation for new members. Classes cannot fulfill that responsibility, however, until they become functioning centers of concern and nurture. Each class should strive to be in miniature what they want the church to be as a whole. Genuine Christian community does not just happen. People must take responsibility for the needs of each other. The shape of that responsibility within a Sunday school class can be seen in the group charged with caring for those members who are ill. It can be seen in the celebration of birthdays, the arrival of children, grandchildren, or any other significant happenings, or life-changing events within the lives of class members.

Christian concern is demonstrated when there is an organization to follow up on class absentees. Some of the most angry people I know are those who feel rejected because they dropped out of Sunday school over a period of several weeks and no one noticed. Perhaps there had been a death in the family and the class member had neglected to let other class members know about the sadness, but when no one asked over a period of weeks, resentment mounted and the end result is an alienated family who generally transfers its membership. The class must be structured to prevent anyone "slipping through the cracks" and must constantly improve the quality of the care given to its membership.

The most effective method of evangelism is that which wins an individual first to a Sunday School class or to an ongoing group in the life of the church. The church membership that follows becomes a celebration of the love and concern the individual has already found in the smaller group. We cannot, however, successfully enlarge our classes unless there is substance both in the teaching and in the group life of the membership.

In many ways we have deserved the demise of our Sunday school. We have settled for warm bodies in

the classrooms and have made no requirements of
our teachers and have failed to afford them training
and nurture. We have, moreover, taken advantage of
those caring, committed persons who have agreed to
serve as teachers in our Sunday school. We have
locked them into their positions and have expected
them to serve a life term without any support or
nurture for themselves. The only way such locked-in
teachers have managed to get free of their responsibilities was to die, get mad, or move away. Many of
them have, understandably, burned out, gone sour,
or otherwise become ineffective. We need to make a
new beginning in our Sunday school. Any new
beginning should be preceded by a period of
repentance on the part of the pastors for the manner
in which we have treated our volunteers in the past.

Pastors do not have the right to enlist any
volunteer, certainly not a teacher, unless the pastor
can answer some basic questions for the volunteer.
These questions are: When does my responsibility
begin? When does my responsibility end? What is
expected of me? When and where do I receive
training? What are the dates and the times? Where
are the materials I will need? Who will teach me how
to use these materials? Who will sustain me while I
am fulfilling my responsibilities?

If a pastor is not ready to answer all of those
questions, he or she should not issue a ringing
challenge to the people. Constantly motivating
people to respond and then leaving them isolated
and bewildered diminishes their capacity to respond
and adds to their feelings of frustration and
disillusionment. Make the requirements clear. Do
not, however, talk about the requirements without

making the training and the support available for the fulfillment of the responsibilities.

Some years ago, in another church, we began a program called "TnT"—Teachers In Training. That concept proved to be dynamite for our Sunday school. Each time we enlisted teachers, we spelled out the challenge as follows: We asked selected individuals whom we felt had teaching ability, regardless of whether they had ever taught before, to agree to sign up for a minimum of nine months training in teaching. Second, we asked them to agree to be the lead teacher in a classroom for at least one year and no more than two years. At the end of two years, they were required to rotate back into their own classes for a minimum of one year, after which they would be eligible to teach again if they desired. On the same card spelling out these requirements, we placed the date, the place, and the time for their first training session.

The trainees then combined to form a separate Sunday school class. The class not only learned something about the use of denominational materials, the centrality of the Scriptures and how to teach the Bible, effective teaching techniques, and many other helpful items, but they also learned how to incarnate Christian community. During the nine-month training session, the group was relieved of any other heavy responsibilities in the church and was given a syllabus of required readings to aid them in their teaching preparations. Far from shrinking from such stringent requirements, we discovered at least twenty-five people in that church of 1,200 persons who were eager to learn how to teach, provided someone would teach them before they were assigned to a class.

Toward the end of the nine months of training, class members engaged in "student teaching" and were videotaped as they taught. Mannerisms and teaching techniques were discussed in detail. Their graduation was observed by the entire congregation, and they were presented during the primary 11:00 service. As a part of their recognition, they were publicly assigned by the Work Area on Education to their classes. The trained teachers were received with such enthusiasm, that those classes whose teachers had not been trained began to insist that theirs go for the same training that they saw and heard in the newly trained teachers. The end result of the experiment was that the Administrative Board requested the Work Area on Education to see that all teachers were trained prior to letting them teach on the faculty of the Sunday school. We went from a position in that church where teachers were being recruited from the halls and vestibules, where practically any willing warm body was acceptable, to a church where people had to sign up on a waiting list if they wanted to teach.

The results in the church school where the teachers were adequately trained were simply amazing. The Sunday school attendance began to increase in direct relationship to the growing church attendance, and the membership of the church began to grow in almost direct relationship to growth of the Sunday school. As a matter of fact, 95 percent of the members were coming into the church by way of the Sunday school. When they joined the church, they were already deeply involved in their Sunday school classes and groups and no one had to worry about assimilation. Sunday school attendance nearly doubled over a period of a few years, and the church membership began to grow at an annual growth rate that would double its active membership every five years. The pastor, moreover, was relieved from having to carefully cultivate each new member because that important work was being shared by numerous youth and adult classes that were reaching out to newcomers.

An important aspect of congregational care is the preservation of church membership. In most churches, the attendance at the worship services is far greater than those persons who are in attendance at Sunday school. This means, of course, unless there is definite intentional follow-up on absentees in worship, there is no mechanism in place to prevent persons from dropping out and simply being lost in the shuffle. Sunday school classes, with their nurturing committees intact, can keep up with their constituents, particularly if the class is kept in manageable proportions. Effective congregational care will, just as the Sunday school, keep up with members of the church. Many of our churches are taking advantage of the inexpensive personal computers to keep up with their attendance records. Utilizing the attendance forms, those records are checked by the personal computer each Sunday to determine which members have been absent for, say, three consecutive Sundays.

The committee charged with this responsibility should not be expected to deal with the entire roll of the church, including out-of-town, long-term inactives. The church can, instead, choose several

Sundays, perhaps even including an Easter Sunday
or a Christmas Sunday when the crowd is unusually
good, and start with those persons who are at least
measurably active. A number is assigned to those
persons, although the congregation never knows
that that number has been assigned, and the
committee can quickly insert the numbers into the
personal computer and get a printout showing
which persons have been absent for several consecutive Sundays.

Such computers are accessible to most of our
churches, but even if one is not available, such
records can be handled quickly by hand by a
dedicated volunteer. I know of one retired individual
who kept up with the attendance of his church by
setting aside Monday for that purpose. His church
had a membership of 1,800, of which about 900 were
considered active. When a computer has been
programmed to show the names, addresses, and
telephone numbers of the members, it becomes a
very simple procedure for several volunteers to
quickly call those persons who have been absent for
three consecutive weeks.

As is the case with all volunteers, no one should be
expected to serve in the area of congregational care
without training. Callers will have been instructed to
make a friendly call to the absentees. There should
not be, for instance, any negative or guilt-inducing
calls. There should be a sincere sound of Christian
concern accompanying some questions about the
family's well-being. When the call is of the proper
kind, recipients receive it with gratitude and that
warm feeling that comes with the realization that
they are missed; therefore they are important

members of the church. When a family is consistently absent from church over a period of weeks, no
matter how valid or invalid their reasons for absence,
and no one follows through with a note or a
telephone call, that family will join the permanent
ranks of the inactives or will transfer altogether. A
task force on the preservation of church membership, when properly instructed, can significantly
increase church attendance and can contribute
greatly to the well-being of the congregation's life.

When attendance records are used to keep up with
the attendance of the congregation, the registration
of one's attendance becomes more than a means to
get the names and addresses of visitors and
prospects. Registering attendance takes on a greater
meaning when the church sincerely wishes to keep
up with its people and to demonstrate genuine
concern when they are absent. The larger the
church becomes, the more crucial such ministry
becomes. Small churches must not, however, take
for granted that someone is following up on the
absentees.

Another key component that places a church in a
position to grow is the congregation's realization of
the possibilities for doing mission in the local
community. We must constantly be vigilant to
instruct the people concerning the nature of
Christian mission. In our connectional system, it is
easy for uninformed members to think of missions in
terms of something "out there." Our connectional
system, for all its great strengths, also has some
dangers within it. One of the dangers is that through
our giving to benevolences, or to apportionments, we
become convinced that we are paying someone else

to do our mission work for us. In order to be vital, however, the local church must have missions personalized to the degree that people who come there seeking inner holiness may know that here is a community in which they can find expression for that holiness in outer service.

One of the key task forces in any local church is a work area on missions. Not only do they have the responsibility to constantly interpret and inform the congregation concerning the international and national picture as our church confronts the world with the claims of Jesus Christ, but that work area must also creatively involve the people in the expression of their mission concern on the local level. I have discovered that support for apportionments diminishes in direct relationship to the lack of involvement on the part of the people on the local scene.

One of the most exciting developments in The United Methodist Church in recent years has been the volunteers in mission program (VIM). Countless churches have been turned around in terms of mission involvement through lay persons who have gone as short-term volunteers to actually do the work of missions with their own hands, or have found the needs of people in their own community. Their experience, when communicated with excitement to the congregation, is contagious and fires the purpose of missions in every local church that has supported such teams. While some mission work is tedious and complex and should be approached only by those who are well-versed and trained in that culture with its specific needs, it is regrettable that in recent years missions have somehow excluded the

average lay person. Our laity have many skills, and
they are more affluent and have more time to give
than ever before in the history of our church. It is
most unfortunate that their willingness to serve as
short-term volunteers has not been eagerly em-
braced by some of the persons responsible for such
programs in the denomination of which I am a part.
We have only now begun, and reluctantly so, to
create a place for volunteers in mission and to
officially recognize it as an authentic expression of
mission in The United Methodist Church.

One of the dangers related to missions has to do
with our ever-increasing apportionments. Actually
the amount given to apportionments by the average
United Methodist is appallingly small. When the
budget crunch comes down (now occurring with
greater frequency), it is the local mission effort that
almost always gives way to the church-wide
apportionments many of us rightfully insist on
paying in full.

Some years ago, in the South Georgia conference, a study was conducted relative to the
increase of local church budgets, the increase of
average salaries in the locale, and the increase of
apportionments both on a conference and national
level. The study revealed that the apportionments
were going up most rapidly on the annual
conference level, secondly on the national level,
and in both cases they were far outstripping the
increase of the overall church budget and the
increase in salaries. That conference made some
recommendations concerning the increases because it was obvious from the study that the trend
could not continue.

I am not making a plea for the reduction of apportionments as much as I am expressing a concern that budgets be rearranged to put high priority on permitting the people to personalize their mission efforts through engagement on the local level. The ability to start mission churches and other significant projects on the local level is a wonderful technique, not only to extend the kingdom, but to generate great excitement within the local church. Where there is excitement on the local level, enthusiasm for the payment of apportionments that go beyond the annual conference level increases and the whole church profits.

There are many large churches in the city of Houston, Texas. There are many large Baptist churches, Presbyterian churches, United Methodist churches and others. Several of the large Baptist churches are mothering small mission churches with phenomenal growth. The success of those "out-post" churches not only contributes to the growth of the denomination, but actually galvanizes and excites the mother church. In the case of our United Methodist churches, our connectional system does not give us the leeway to make such extraordinary expenditures on the local level. While we are organized to begin new churches, it seems always to be happening "out there," so that the full impact of having been a part of a significant beginning is lost on the rank and file member of the local church. I do not know of a single church in our city that gives more money to missions than ours. However, in spite of the best education we can give, including mission saturation weekends, we cannot begin to affect our congregation as completely as we would like unless our program also includes some rather dramatic efforts on the local level. We must be sensitive to the need to reserve a large portion of our mission dollar for the mission needs on our local doorstep.

While I believe that key components must come together in order to position the church for growth, the underlying assumption is that such components combine to convince the people in the pew that *they are the church.* Our people must realize that it is our church. We cannot look to Nashville, to New York, or to any other place to fix the problems within our denomination. If we have learned anything at all from books such as *Megatrends,* we have been reassured that anything that comes from the top down must be classified as a fad. Only that which comes from the grass roots upward can be categorized as a trend. "They" will not fix our church or solve its problems. We would do well to heed the words written on the gates of the Wisemann Institute in Tel Aviv. In the beginning days of the infant nation of Israel, a wise person put on the gates of that prominent institution, "Look not to the kings of the east or to the kings of the west, but to your own hands." We must begin to look to our own hands.

Involve the Congregation

When I first arrived in Houston as the pastor of First United Methodist Church, a reporter asked me what my goals were for the congregation. I replied that the first thing I wanted to do was to find out what the people of God wanted to do for Christ in that community and to discover how I could help them do it. I believe that the process of listening, whether we do it by cluster groups or listening posts, is the first step toward getting all of the people involved. Another name for this involvement is *ownership*. When we listen to the people as they share their goals and aspirations for their church and then help them through process planning to put them into shape and form, finally undergirding them with financial support and people power, the church becomes theirs in the truest sense. Then the budgets begin to go up dramatically and the people start to make themselves available for service because they see their ideas (no doubt sometimes reshaped and defined), but nevertheless their hopes and their dreams coming back at them as the program of the church. Nothing can substitute for ownership.

A goal in which every congregation should share is the establishment of a membership recruitment figure. Each congregation should be asked "How many new members should we receive and assimilate into our fellowship next year?" The pastor can, through the use of conference journals, quickly determine how many new members are required in order to maintain the numerical strength of the church and how many new members would be required in order to facilitate aggressive growth. Generally a 10 percent increase is representative of genuine growth of the kind we need in our denomination. This goal should be agreed upon by the Work Area on Evangelism, then the Council on Ministries, and finally the Administrative Board and the Charge Conference.

Once the growth goal has been agreed upon by the pastor and the congregation, it becomes the responsibility of the pastor and the church leaders to educate the congregation as to the intentional and purposeful methods available to them that will help the church grow.

Congregations should be quickly made aware of the futility of simply waiting for new members to walk into the church. Studies have shown that less than 10 percent of our new members come that way. The church, especially downtown churches or those located in an obscure or remote area, cannot survive if they merely wait for the chance visitor. The congregation must accept the burden of the responsibility of cultivating and inviting prospective members to their church.

In my former church, as well as my present one, I have been keeping a record of those new members who simply happen to walk into the church. In both cases, the number is so small as to be almost nonexistent. Many of our new members were introduced to the church by the televised service of worship or through the radio. Through the powerful medium of television, people become psychologically linked to a congregation and come to know its worship leaders on a rather intimate basis. Once that linkage has been established, it is usually only a matter of time before such persons come to visit the church in person if their proximity to the church makes this possible. Many of those persons, if warmly welcomed by the congregation, will ultimately become members of the church.

We are becoming increasingly aware of what a powerful tool television can be for the recruitment of new members. Any congregation with a cable system nearby or even a low-power television station should make every effort to get at least a portion of their service televised. If the financial resources are not available for television, perhaps radio time can be purchased. Neither of these mediums should be underestimated or overlooked by a church eager to spread its influence and to grow. Our large downtown church is fully aware of our great dependence upon television. We are committed to that ministry no matter what the cost.

Some weeks ago my wife and I were returning to Texas on an interstate highway during the Sunday morning worship hour. I had officiated at a Saturday night wedding in a distant state. We found ourselves at church time with no church in sight. Not wanting to take the time to try to find a church service on the radio, I pulled into a nearby motel and asked those persons in the lobby to direct me to their favorite worship service on the radio. I did not tell them that I was a Methodist pastor. I simply asked if anyone had a favorite worship service to which they listened on Sunday morning. There were several persons in that motel lobby, and each of them had a favorite. The consensus was interestingly enough a United Methodist Church in a city about fifty miles from where we were presently located. As I returned to the car and located the worship service on my radio dial, I reflected on the fact that every person in that motel lobby was apparently a regular listener to a service of worship on the radio. Probably not all of them were regular worshipers in a local congregation, but all of them worship by radio.

We have many congregations. There are those who are diligent in their listening habits who never darken the door of our local church. While the church must be caring for its own membership, it must also extend its caring to those who are outside its walls. The message of the Gospel is for all persons. Even the smallest church can oftentimes find free time on the radio or time on the radio at a very nominal cost. Each church must make every effort to broaden its audience and expand its pulpit through radio and television.

Through the questionnaire which we issue to our new members, we have failed to discover anyone who has joined the church purely as a result of newspaper advertising. Many times I am persuaded that church people like to see their ad in the paper for their sakes more than for the sake of the un-churched. Such newspaper promotion undoubtedly is of value especially when promoting special services, sermon series, or musical occasions. As just a weekly effort, however, we have decided that the weekly ad in the newspaper has not been that effective for us.

The most effective method and means of doing evangelism is available to every church no matter its size. Its most precious resource is the active members of the congregation. Through preaching and teaching, the congregation must be brought to the realization that in our Protestant understanding of the priesthood of believers, their baptism consti-tutes an ordination to do the work of evangelism. It is not enough for a charge conference to agree on the number of persons who should be brought into the church during a given year. The congregation must never be permitted to set a goal and then sit back to see whether the paid staff can pull it off. Evangelism for too long has been contingent on the preacher's ability to chase moving vans and follow up new-comers with the right questions that enable them to say yes to having their names put on the church rolls. Effective evangelism becomes a reality when the entire congregation begins to become inten-tional about realizing its membership goals.

In order for a congregation to be intentional about growing, there must be a time, a place, and an opportunity for the congregation at large to make a definite commitment to doing its part toward reaching the goal. I have found a commitment card extremely helpful in the recruitment of people (who says the only commitment card should be for church budgets?) Such commitment cards give conscientious people an opportunity to make their concern real and visible first of all before the altar of the church and the entire family of God, and then fortifies them with that public commitment as they make their concern real in the world.

Epiphany Sunday is the day we have chosen to call the entire congregation to a involvement in evangelism. Preparations for that climactic Sunday begin, of course, weeks before the actual call is issued from the pulpit. The call to make a commitment can never be issued until the entire congregation is well-informed regarding the nature of the commitment they are being called to make. What is being required of each volunteer should be publicized through every means available to the local church. As the program moves into its second and third year, testimonials can be very effective in the recruitment of workers. Those who have had growing experiences in the work of evangelism can profitably share for a few minutes in Sunday school classes, in the pulpit and any other place where the congregation gathers. In addition to the general publicity that accompanies a massive effort of the kind I am describing, personal letters should also be sent to key leaders of the church, such as the Administrative Board, Sunday school presidents, Sunday school teachers, Council on Ministries work area chairpersons, and so on. (A sample letter of the kind we have used is included at the end of this chapter.)

Specific challenges to become involved in evangelism should also be issued to those who are the newest members of the congregation. New members bring new members. They represent relative circles, friendship circles, recreation circles, work circles that are outside the bounds of the congregation and are, therefore, filled with new possibilities for membership recruitment. There should be, therefore, an intentional effort to include the newest members of the church in that group that will be publicly called to the altar on Epiphany Sunday.

What shall we call those persons who are challenged to become intentional in their commitment to make the church grow? In one particular church where I was pastor, there had been a "Committee of One Hundred" that had stood in the gap in a crucial time in the life of that congregation when the sanctuary was being built. Because the members of that committee had been pivotal in its early years, the committee was always spoken of with a great deal of respect and admiration. When the Council on Ministries of that particular congregation chose to set a membership growth goal of one hundred for the ensuing year, it was only natural that we should call the group the "Committee of One Hundred." This also coincided with our belief that the church should experience a 10 percent membership gain during the course of the year in order to demonstrate aggressive growth. One may simply use the idea of the committee and make it the committee of whatever the membership goal is for that year. Some who have engaged in similar efforts have called it "Operation Andrew." Each congregation can, of course, be creative in selecting the name for those important persons who commit themselves to do the work of evangelism.

Each member of the committee should agree to the following:

1. To try their very best (an effort goal) to win one person to Christ and to his church during that calendar year.

2. Agree to attend two banquets during the course of the year (the dates of which are already set at the time the person is recruited). The first banquet will have to do with inspiration and instruction, and will be held within two weeks after the recruitment Sunday. The second banquet, which has to do with celebration and testimonials, will be held in December, and those dates should also be included on the commitment card that the committee member signs.

3. Each member agrees to pray for other members of the committee by name each day. Consequently, each person is given a list containing the names of all of the other committee members. These lists are broken down into small groups to be prayed for daily.

A further word should be spoken about the place of prayer. When we ask our people to promise to support the church with their "prayers, presence, gifts, and service," I do not think it accidental that their first promise is to support the church with their prayers. All the rest of the responses are, I believe, predicated upon the first. When someone begins to be intentional with their prayer support, then all of their other support follows. We ask all persons engaged in the work of evangelism to pray for each other by name. When they turn in their commitment cards, we give them post cards on which they are to write the names of those whom they have chosen to cultivate. Those cards are addressed to the work area on prayer. This work area, which is named and organized just as other required work areas in the church, has the responsibility of bathing those persons named by the committee members in their prayers. Our work area on prayer, which has a large number of volunteer prayer captains, assumes responsibility for praying for those who are cultivating new members and for those who are the prospective new members. The entire effort is an acknowledgement that the prevenient grace of God is at work in every human heart and all of our prayer efforts are an attempt to help God get his way in the life of his people.

Incidentally, the work area on prayer prays for each member of our congregation on her or his birthday and always includes members who are hospitalized and who have suffered grief. The work area on prayer is available for prayer through request cards to the entire congregation for any special needs.

All persons are reminded that their term of service is for one year. They are, of course, urged to sign up again the following Epiphany Sunday and to renew their commitment to the work of evangelism. The entire congregation should be constantly reminded that assuming responsibility for church growth is not to be considered on the level with a "committee assignment," but is the "rent" all Christians pay for the space they take up within the life of the church of Christ. It is the continuing work of every baptized Christian.

Much of the effectiveness of the challenge to
become involved in evangelism can be traced to the
pulpit. After all of the preparation, the prayers and
the publicity, the preacher must get the people to
realize through the sermon that they are the answer
to the prayer of our Master who prayed that God
would send forth laborers into his harvest. The
preacher must be clear concerning God's expectation for his people, and the sermon must throb with
the very passion of Christ who rejoiced to see one lost
person saved.

Initial recruitment may be difficult because
although the assignment is made clear and the
training is also made available, winning another
person to Christ and his church is an imposing
responsibility. The effectiveness of the recruitment
should, however, increase with each passing year
and generally does in direct proportion to the quality
and amount of followthrough on the part of the
pastor and the work area on evangelism. Although
only a small portion of the congregation may respond
to the acceptance of specific responsibilities, all
members of the church should be urged to become
good will ambassadors by saying a positive word on
behalf of their church, its program, its ministry, and
its mission at least several times each week. The
climate for growth is established once church
members begin to say positive things about their
church. It is only a short step from that posture of
positive statements to the assumption of specific
responsibility in the area of church growth.

Now let us speak specifically about the followup
for those who have chosen to be intentional and
purposeful in winning other persons to Christ and to

his church. I am thinking now about the initial banquet, held within two weeks following Epiphany Sunday when the people have brought their commitment cards to the altar and have been recognized by the pastor and the congregation as those who have accepted responsibility for making their church grow during that calendar year.

A part of the appeal for involvement in the work of evangelism should contain the thought that this is not just another committee or task force in the life of the church. Evangelism is always the chief responsibility of the total church. Our people are not being called to "busy work" or to an assortment of meetings that will infringe on their family time. Having only two formal meetings per year relative to their evangelism assignment is especially attractive to those who want to help their church grow but do not want to be inundated with meetings. It becomes all the more important, therefore, that the pastor and the work area on evangelism plan that initial banquet in such a way as to use every available moment. I believe persons who attend the banquet are familiar with the need of the church to grow or they would not have committed themselves to its growth. I believe, therefore, three things should happen at that banquet. First of all, the people should be given some idea as to where to look for prospective members. Second, they should be given some suggestions as to how they might cultivate someone into membership within the group life, and finally, the total life of the congregation. Third, they should be given some word of inspiration by the pastor or another speaker to send them on their way.

Where do we look to find a prospect? The Bible says that Andrew first found Simon, his brother. We can begin our search in the most intimate circle of all, the family circle. Just as Andrew started among his relatives, even so our people should be encouraged to check within their families to see whether or not anyone of them is unchurched. A second circle of contacts is, of course, to be found in our friendship circle.

Once I was playing golf with a new friend and during the course of the afternoon I mentioned the name of a member of the church I was serving. The person with whom I was playing opened his eyes wide in amazement and asked, "Is he a member of your congregation?" I told him that he had been a member for many years. My new friend then said that he had been playing golf with our member for several years and had never once heard him mention the fact that he was a member of the church. This does not imply that my church member was not being a moral and ethical person. It does mean that in his circle of friends he is not intentional enough when it comes to sharing a good word about his church. Members should be helped to understand that a seed can be planted on a golf course, at a luncheon meeting, at a business meetng, when you are sitting beside someone on a plane, a bus, in a car—wherever you are and wherever they are. If the polls are accurate, many of the friends of our members are simply waiting for someone to invite them to a church. We must sensitize our members to the possibilities for growth within their friendship circle.

The friendship circle should also be extended to include those persons whom members meet at work and at play. The recreational and the social circles are rich with possibilities for church growth. One church I know gave an evangelism award each year to the lay member who had been judged most effective in bringing other persons into the fellowship of the church. One year the recipient was a thirteen-year-old girl, a member of the church youth group. She had effectively cultivated and brought to the church a physician and his entire family. When I asked the doctor about how the teenager had influenced him to come downtown to that church, he responded by saying that she was his babysitter. Each time he picked her up to sit with his children and took her back home she was enthusiastically telling him about her youth group, the choir, the program, and the spiritual life retreats. He saw in her radiant countenance and in her enthusiasm those qualities which he wanted for his own children. Finally he came to the conclusion that he wanted to rear his children in the same church where his babysitter had found her contagious joy. That Christian young person used her babysitting as a vehicle for doing evangelism.

Everyone can cultivate someone. It is not enough, however, to simply talk about the various circles in which the prospect must be found. We must go beyond that and tell our people how the work of cultivation actually occurs. There are, of course, a multitude of people in our world who are simply waiting to be warmly invited to a Sunday school class, a Bible study or to a service of worship. Many more, however, must be cared about and loved before they commit themselves even to a small group, let alone to the church. Most people need to know that someone genuinely cares for them, and in order to have those feelings they must experience genuine friendship first and then someone can talk to them about church membership. People don't want to be another statistic, nor do they want to be another "victory," a statistic someone can claim. They want to know that they matter. They want to experience genuine warmth and the supportive fellowship that is to be found within the group life of the church.

In order for that to happen, the person who is doing the cultivation must build some bridges, that is, establish some points of contact, points of common interest—hobbies, sports, and such. Sometimes bringing someone into your recreation circle is an effective way of making friends. Something natural has to happen between you and another person before anything supernatural can happen. Talk to anyone about how he or she came to be a church member and more than likely you will discover some individual who was personally appealing and through that person's appeal, the church became appealing.

The Sunday school attendance at my first church averaged in the middle forties. Almost next door to the parsonage was a large family, the father of which I could not interest in Sunday school. I had invited him repeatedly, and my constant invitations had begun to annoy him to the point that when he saw me coming he would look the other way or otherwise avoid me. Recognizing the futility of that approach, I decided to try another. I took him and his family on as a kind of project. I had numbers in my eyes and knew if I could successfully win that family

I would increase my Sunday school attendance by 10 percent. Quite by accident one day, I discovered that my neighbor was an avid frog hunter—reportedly the best frog gigger in that part of the country. Many Saturday nights he and his family feasted on frog legs.

One afternoon I saw him out in his back yard chopping wood for the fireplace. Somehow I managed to approach him on his backside and to speak to him before he could dodge the preacher who had pestered him so long about church attendance. This time I surprised him by asking about where I could get a mess of frog legs. Completely surprised by my question, he stood for a moment as almost in shock and then lit up like a Christmas tree and said, "Why, I go frog gigging every Friday night and I'll be glad to take you along." That Friday night and every Friday night after that for a long time, he and I went frog hunting.

One Sunday I looked up and saw my frog hunting buddy sitting on the back row of my church with all of his family. One Sunday not long afterward I gave the invitation to Christian discipleship, and my friend came down the aisle. In a real sense I knew that that man, who later became the lay leader in his church, had been frog gigged into the church.

The question is quite simple: Do we care enough about people to go out of our way to be their friend, to establish a relationship? Nobody wants to be manipulated. People deserve the right to be with a Christian in order to "judge our stuff." They want to know us; they don't want to see us just on Sunday morning in our Sunday best. They want to know what kind of person we are all week long. They want to see Christians in a different setting in order to evaluate our authenticity and to determine whether or not what we talk about in worship is, in reality, who and where we are. People have a right to that. When they experience real friendship first and then when a friend talks to them about church membership, it has meaning. Many times people must be comfortable with us before they can be comfortable with our church.

Although my motives had not been of the highest in cultivating my neighbor, through the process of becoming friends, he quickly became more than just another statistic. We became such good friends that whether or not he had elected to join my church, our friendship would have still been real. In reality, I have cultivated a number of persons who have never chosen to unite with my church. My own life has, however, been greatly enriched through the contribution of persons with whom I share a very close friendship, but who are still outside the gathered congregation of Christ.

Once I went duck hunting with three individuals whom I had been cultivating for church involvement. I had been largely unsuccessful, but our friendship was growing. We had chosen to go hunting on a bitterly cold afternoon when the ice had formed around the edges of the pond. The ducks began to swarm in and in the excitement of shooting so many times, I forgot myself, stood up in the boat and leaned a little bit too far backward. I promptly went head over heels into the icy water! My hunting companions managed to fish me out of the water although I was heavily weighted with ammunition. The new preacher was a bit bedraggled as they dragged me into the boat and hustled me off to a heater because my wet clothing was already getting icy. They enjoyed a hearty laugh at my expense. In fact, they laughed all the way to my church. In our duck hunting experience, we gained some common ground. Something happened between us. We made a memory. We had enough common ground to be able to say, "Do you remember when . . .?"

I have used the stories of the duck hunt and the frog hunt because I am an outdoorsman and enjoy sports of all kinds. There are lonely people all around us who are waiting to be invited into our world so they might experience something with us that will make us another friend. When there is warmth, concern, and genuine friendship, an invitation to one's Sunday school class is not manipulation, nor does it pose so great a threat to the one who has stood for a long time outside the Christian community.

One further word about the personal cultivation of prospective members. Earlier I mentioned briefly a diary for prospective members in order to guard against self-deception and carelessness. The diary may be no more than a 3-by-5 card someone carries in his or her pocket. It should contain the record of when the last telephone contact was made, when a letter was written, or when the individual was invited to a pot luck dinner, a ball game, or a duck hunt. If we are going to care about people, we must have some kind of systematic plan for our caring. I am constantly amazed at how quickly the weeks, even months, can speed by without our having made an additional contact with someone whom we are cultivating. A diary saves us from such carelessness. I do not, of course, mean by these contacts that we are in any way pestering or badgering someone into a friendship. I do mean that we are all in need of more friends and that Christ, himself, has called us to be concerned about all persons.

One individual comes to mind whom I cultivated for almost two years before he and his family joined our church. I still recall the contact which made the difference in terms of that individual making a commitment to the church. I had carried with me, as I always do when I am traveling, the names and addresses of those persons whom I am cultivating. While en route to a city in Tennessee, I passed through the village where one of my prospects in Houston, Texas, was born. Just as soon as I arrived at my destination in Tennessee, I wrote my prospect a note telling him that I had seen his hometown and could easily understand why he loved it so much. I did not mention anything about joining the church, but the following Sunday my friend came forward, together with his family. He had responded to my invitation to join the church and to commit his life to Christ. I shall never forget what he said to me on that Sunday morning. While the tears were streaming down his cheeks, this imposing man of over six feet said, "Thank you for not giving up on me." Over the course of those almost two years, I had made a minimum of twenty-eight contacts with that individual. That morning, however, all of them were well worth it. Not only did I receive a new member into the body of Christ, but I made what I believe is a lifelong friend.

Perhaps one of the most important words to be said about the cultivation of friends and prospective members for our churches, is a word about the

posture we church people should assume. At all
times we should remember that we are those who
are saved but who are also being saved. All of this is
another way of saying we are sinners too. We have
found something significant in our relationship to
Christ and to the church, and while it is true that
those who have not yet made a commitment to the
fellowship of Christ need something which we have,
it is similarly true that they also have something
which we need. Such recognition negates any
temptation to assume a superior stance toward
anyone. The ground is level at the foot of the cross,
and if we would draw close to anyone, we must put
him or her at complete ease regarding a lack of
judgmentalism on our part. It is instructive for us
that Jesus showed a remarkable ability to put people
at ease. Sinners, those outside the orthodox faith,
were especially comfortable with Christ. He did not
leave them where he found them, but he did put
them at ease by letting them know that he valued
them and the contribution they were capable of
making to the work of his kingdom. He asked the
woman at the well, for instance, to give him a drink
of water. He began the conversation by asking
something of her. That approach within itself caused
her to know that she was valued for her own unique
contribution. She was, therefore, perfectly willing
and eager to hear when he began to speak with her
about what he could offer her in the way of living
water. We do not have all of the answers, nor is our
role that of answer people. We have found mercy.
We have found a way to establish priorities and a
strength that helps us face our adversities. Our way
of understanding ultimate reality, moreover, brings

us joy and gives us peace even in the middle of pain. All of these qualities the world will eagerly embrace, I believe, when the posture of the person presenting them assumes a position of equality, respect, and true concern.

We should not understand ourselves as those who are always giving out something whether money, advice, or answers. We must also learn how to be graceful receivers. We must not exclusively claim the blessings that giving always provides. We must share such blessings with those who also have something to give, even though they stand outside the redemptive fellowship of the church. To recognize such capacity on the part of unchurched persons is to accord that respect which is essential to the establishment of any genuine relationship.

January 4, 1985

Mr. and Mrs. John Doe
234 W. 5th St.
Any City, USA 00000

Dear Mary and John,

One of the big moments in our ministry this year will be when I call for volunteers in the work area on evangelism at the Sunday morning services on January 13. I am praying that at the conclusion of those services one thousand people will come forward agreeing to:

1. Do his/her very best to bring one new member into the church during 1985.

2. Attend one Training and Inspiration Banquet on Saturday, January 26 at 7:30 P.M.

3. Attend one Celebration Banquet on December 15 at 7:30 P.M.

4. Pray daily for each person involved in this endeavor.

This One in a Thousand mission will not in any way hinder your other service projects! As you know, this is not another committee—we have but two meetings per year.

Will you give prayerful consideration to joining Jean Smith, Rick Anderson, and me in this vital effort? Please help lead the way when I issue the call on January 13.

I believe you are *one in a thousand!*

In Him,

William H. Hinson

P.S. Commitment cards will be available in the bulletin Sunday morning.

Win the Visitors

The church that depends on "walk in" prospects for its membership growth will steadily decline. Real growth requires intentional cultivation on the part of the entire membership. We cannot, however, neglect that 5 to 10 percent of our members who do simply walk into the sanctuary uninvited. Many such walk-ins are transplanted members—average church members—who are a part of the national average, in that their job requires them to move once every five years. If an average career spans forty years, the average United Methodist will more than likely move eight times. One of the continuing burdens of the church is that many of our members must be won or reclaimed again and again. We must devise a method and an organization for securing the church membership of transplanted Christians quickly and efficiently. Such an effective plan can free the church from at least a portion of its preoccupation of rewinning already committed Christians so that it may engage in the larger work of cultivation that results in first-time commitments. This chapter is about a plan for responding to the first-time visitors who simply walk into the service of worship.

The ushers in any church are extremely important people. They are oftentimes those who make the first impression on visitors. Since first impressions are very important, ushers should be carefully trained in all of the responsibility attendant to their office. Many churches no longer just rely on the ushers who stand at the door of the sanctuary, but also recruit and train outside ushers who greet the people as they are coming into the parking lot or walking across the street toward the church. In many situations, such persons serve as effective guides for the directing of traffic and pointing out available parking spaces to those who are unfamiliar with the surroundings. Such ushers are especially welcome when the weather is rainy, and they can be there with large umbrellas to escort persons into the church. Persons with handicapping conditions are especially grateful for the cheerful assistance of those who are well-trained in caring for them. I cannot overemphasize the importance of these ambassadors of good will.

In addition to thoughtful, helpful ushers, every church must cultivate a warm, friendly spirit among the people in the pew. We are blessed in our church in that we have long standing members who act as chaplains to the sections in which they regularly sit while worshiping. Not only do these persons keep up with all of the regulars who worship in that section, but they also spot any new persons who are present and they make sure that those newcomers are warmly welcomed. Let me tell you a story about one such chaplain.

Some months ago a young woman came into our church fifteen minutes before the service of worship was scheduled to begin. She had never worshiped in our church before, and on that Sunday she made her way to one of the sections where the chaplain happens to be an 86-year-old woman. As soon as the young woman sat down, our chaplain slipped over beside her, patted her hand, introduced herself, and said, "I'm so glad you came to worship in our church today."

Following the service, other friendly persons began to speak to the young woman and the next Sunday she was back again, sitting in the same section. A few weeks later she came forward when the invitation was issued and became a part of our fellowship. Later, just before she had finished her Ph.D. in chemistry, she responded to the claim of God on her life for the Christian ministry.

While speaking to her one day, I asked that brilliant young woman when the change began that was so dramatic in her life. She responded by saying that it started for her that Sunday morning when she came alone, nervous, and a little bit anxious to our sanctuary and one of our women came, patted her hand, and made her feel at home.

"In a real sense," the young woman said, "I felt that on that morning I had come home." Nothing can take the place of people who are committed to making strangers feel at home.

Attendance registration is absolutely essential. The passing of such registration forms in our churches should be viewed as a friendship ritual that enables us to be responsive and warm toward those persons seated beside us. Such registration is an excellent way to learn the names of other church members as well as to discover the names and addresses of those who are visiting. The registration of attendance is also invaluable because of the congregational care task force who are charged with the responsibility of following up on absentees. Church members also may use these registration forms to request a visit from the pastor or to indicate address changes or any other needs that should be transmitted to the church office.

Immediately following the morning service of worship, the committee on the work area on evangelism collects all of the registration forms in the pews and circles the names of the visitors. The visitors are then divided into the category of first-time visitors, second-time, third-time, etc. Such records can be kept easily on a personal computer, or lacking a computer, an alphabetized journal can be kept containing the names, addresses, and number of times persons have visited the church. First-time visitors are set aside and their telephone numbers are placed beside their names. In the registration of attendance forms which we use, there is a place for the telephone numbers to be given and if the old-time church member is willing to complete the forms, a majority of the visitors will also oblige in giving all of the information requested, including telephone numbers for the work place as well as the residence number.

During the afternoon following the person's visit, the pastor or someone trained by the pastor should telephone all of the first-time visitors and extend to them a personal word of welcome. (Some pastors prefer to have the visitors stand in the service and to address them personally while they stand. In the churches I have served, I have found that to be poorly received both by the membership and the person being spotlighted. I choose instead to welcome them by way of the telephone on the very afternoon when they have visited in the morning.) Not only should first-time visitors receive a telephone call from the pastor or a special welcoming committee, but they should also be visited by members of the church on the very afternoon when they visited the church.

Each church should recruit enough persons to visit all of those individuals who visit the church each Sunday. Such church visitors can, by careful training, become specialists in visitation. They must be carefully chosen, trained, and challenged to give one afternoon per month for church visitation. They must also agree to spend an entire weekend in intensive training for such important visitation.

I have found that a retreat setting is most effective for the training of visitation specialists. Discipleship Resources of the Board of Discipleship of the United Methodist Church, Nashville, Tennessee, has a wealth of materials that can be used effectively in training such volunteers. Perhaps the most effective of the various techniques I have used is to take the volunteers on a kind of faith pilgrimage. In taking that pilgrimage, I encourage them to identify those persons in their life experiences who have stood in the gap for them. I ask them to describe those important persons in one or two words.

After we have shared a number of words and experiences, I then lead the group through some biblical accounts of conversions and dramatic life-changing situations and help them to see that what they experienced through a friend or a family member was, in reality, the same grace, love, acceptance, and forgiveness so dramatically presented in the Scriptures. Then we talk about how we can make those words concrete in our relationships with those whom we meet in a home visit. Finally, the group engages in a great deal of role playing, involving every conceivable situation. The basic information needed from the telephone call to the first-time visitor is discussed and sought in such role-playing situations until it becomes second nature for the visitors. They determine, for instance, whether or not the visitor knows someone in the congregation and was invited by them. If that is the case, then the prospect is already under the care of one of the cultivators in the congregation, and that person becomes the important contact between the church and the prospective member. The needs of the family with reference to the church can be quickly determined. The grades, ages, and needs of the children, the work place of the parents, the location of their previous home, if they have newly moved to the community, are important information to have.

During the training weekend, the visitation specialists, called the First Wave in our church, talk about all of the reasons why they chose to be members of our church. All of those reasons are strong testimonials that prospective volunteers can readily share with prospective members. The visitation specialists also discuss the types of materials the church offers in the way of information about its program, its Christian Education, and its music. If there is a Wednesday night church supper, a complimentary ticket can be given to the visiting family.

The first people to visit prospective members are so important that their training must be complete and thorough. They should be taught some good public relations principles. They should know when it is inconvenient for them to enter the home and when to spend a half minute or so in engaging a prospective member in conversation outside the front door of their house. They must develop such a sensitive feel for the whole experience of visitation that they can, even under adverse circumstances, leave the prospect with a positive good feeling about the church and its caring representative.

Let me say a word now about how the first-time visitors are assigned to the visitation specialist. In small towns or rural communities, visitation by neighborhoods is ideal. A volunteer can easily find those streets in the vicinity around where she/he lives. Larger communities should recruit volunteers from every zip code so that they may be able to effectively visit persons who live in the same general vicinity where they live. It should be noted that there is special appeal in the church representatives' ability to say to the prospect that he or she lives in the same neighborhood. In large urban areas, we have found that the corridor approach is most effective. With this plan the church becomes the hub and the corridors are like spokes in a wheel going out in every direction from the church. A church member who lives in one of those corridors would visit all of the persons along the path that he or she travels on the way to and from church, which should naturally be familiar terrain for them. There should be a sufficient number of volunteers in order to prevent having to assign a visitor to an unfamiliar corridor of the city.

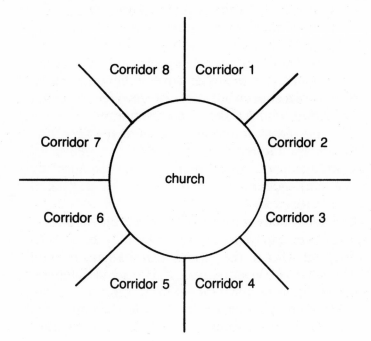

The church visitor makes his or her report to the visitation coordinator on Sunday evening or Monday, at the latest. The coordinator then assigns the prospect to an outreach chairperson in the Sunday school class where the visitor and coordinator think the person would best fit. (Each Sunday school class has an outreach chairperson who receives the names of the prospects from the coordinator.)

Sometime between Wednesday and Saturday, a member of the Sunday school class, hopefully one who lives in the same vicinity as the prospect, personally invites the prospect to his or her class. We encourage our outreach coordinators to have their class members meet the prospect at an easily identified location, or better still to pick them up and give them a ride to Sunday school. No matter what the size of a church building, a stranger trying to find a Sunday school class may find it intimidating. A Sunday school member who simply says to a prospect, "I'll meet you in Room 401 Sunday morning," is not very caring concerning the stranger. One might as well add, "Good luck in finding the room."

Each Sunday school class that has been assigned a prospect receives a form on the following Sunday morning which the outreach chairperson must complete. The visitation coordinator or a member of the evangelism task force circulates the forms and determines whether or not the class has followed through on the invitation and the cultivation of the prospective member.

When the prospect becomes a member of the Sunday school class, his or her membership is noted on the report form and the pastor is notified. The

pastor will, in turn, make an appointment with the
prospect and at that time invite him or her into
church membership. When the transfer is complete,
the new member is presented to the congregation,
and the Sunday school class of which he or she is a
part is encouraged to come and stand with them on
the occasion of their presentation for church
membership. Church membership becomes, then, a
celebration of what the prospect has already found,
that is, a warm, caring, supporting fellowship that
makes disciples rather than simply adding members
to the roles.

Our responsibility does not end, however, when a
prospect chooses to become a member of the church.
We must be diligent in assimilating all new
members. Since we have begun reversing the
process by assimilating people into Sunday school
classes and Bible study groups before their enroll-
ment in the church, I have discovered that the
problems of assimilation have decreased dramatically. Participation in Sunday school attendance,
worship attendance, pledging to the church budget,
and involvement in the church's ministry have gone
up dramatically. Although someone comes into the
fellowship of the church only after being completely
assimilated into the Sunday school fellowship, there
are still some steps that need to be taken in order to
complete assimilation.

All new members are invited to meet with the
pastor and a task force from the stewardship work
area for four consecutive Sundays during the
Sunday school hour. Since the material covered is
the same month after month, it does not matter
when someone begins the four sessions requested

by the pastor. Using key leaders in the church, the program and ministry of the church, and its budget are thoroughly explained. A commitment card is given to the new member, together with some offering envelopes. The church's expectation of the new members is clearly spelled out by the pastor. Service opportunities within the church and the community are discussed at length. The new members' various interests are recorded on a talent sheet and are supplied to the committee on nominations and personnel, and the various work areas on the Council of Ministries. The history of the church and its place in the community is an interesting subject for the new members. The pastor usually leads a discussion on church vows and the future of the church ministry. In addition to a minimum of four orientation classes, a semi-annual course on denominational beliefs should be made available to all new members, especially those new to the denomination. A diligent attempt should be made to help the new member see his or her place in the community of faith.

One of the things I like to do in the closing session with new members is to ask them to place on a 3-by-5 card the name of someone they know who needs to discover what they have found in the church. I encourage them to do that so that we might pray with them about that prospective member in order to help them bring that person into the fellowship. New members consistently bring a great deal of excitement and enthusiasm to the community of faith, and the card I ask them to complete is one attempt to help them capture that enthusiasm and to use it for evangelism. New members generally move in different circles with more unchurched people than regular church members.

Some churches use family sponsor methods in which the new member is assigned to another church member who is responsible for seeing that the newcomer is effectively assimilated into the church community. While that method has proven effective for many churches, I much prefer the method outlined above in which the newcomer is a part of the group life of the church through its Sunday school. If a new member refuses to become involved in any activity other than the principal worship service, perhaps that would be an occasion when a sponsor could be used to good advantage.

We have discovered that the hour before the Sunday evening service of worship is an effective time for the educating and assimilating of new members into the life of the church. Additional classes can be offered then that will not take them out of their Sunday morning Sunday school class. Here are some six-week courses that I have found extremely helpful for assimilating new members. "The Covenant People" is a class where the concept of the covenant is traced through the old and the new testaments. In that course the sacraments of the church are defined and discussed. An attempt is made to help the new member see mission as a natural outgrowth of being a part of the community of faith. "United Methodist Beliefs" is a course offered twice each year. A growing body of materials is available for that course, and we have discovered that many of our long-term members are enjoying that course as well as our newest members. Periodically, we also offer a course on "How To Get the Most out of Your Bible." This course is pretty much patterned after what Harry Emerson Fosdick did in an earlier generation. It is designed to enable our people to avoid many of the excesses into which they often fall in our day. Helps are provided them in the development of a devotional life, and various biblical concepts like progressive revelation are discussed.

Almost always the pastor teaches the courses designed to assist new members in getting grounded in the congregational life. These times together offer a unique opportunity for the pastor to know his or her members on a more intimate basis. I encourage all new members to take at least three of the classes that will help them become better informed members of the church. When a new member has spent eighteen weeks in the company of his or her pastor in a learning situation where give and take is encouraged in each of the class sessions, a relationship has developed in which genuine ministry can occur.

Find the Stamina to Serve

Some months ago, a minister in Mississippi confessed to me that he had been dabbling at the ministry for forty years. At another pastor's school, a superintendent told me that his pastors are consumed with earning CEU credits and drinking coffee. Another leader shared with me in a tone tinged by sarcasm that the greatest need of our church is to overcome the "energy efficiency" of our pastors. The problem of motivationally deprived persons has been screaming at the church for some kind of a solution.

What motivates us? How is it that one pastor cannot rest until all the prospects in his or her parish have been called, while another cannot even make a telephone contact? What is the chief difference between the pastor who spends twenty hours a week in diligent sermon preparation and that one who always prepares a Saturday night special and uses whatever sloppy materials are available?

How can we explain the contrast between a pastor who has great reservoirs of power to listen, to empathize, to visit, to work, and another whose wagon stays loaded, who is always tired? How many of us have stiff-armed people with genuine needs because we are preoccupied with personal problems? Can the differences be explained purely on a secular basis?

Is the motivated pastor driven by a desire for career advancement, a larger church, a bigger salary, or is the difference deeper than that? How does our motivation differ from that of the typical business person?

I believe an unmotivated pastor is a contradiction in terms. We are at one and the same time the most peaceful, but productive persons alive. We have motivators (when we are in touch with them) sufficient to keep us on tiptoe as long as we live.

Jesus believed gratitude was a great and worthy motivator. Once when Jesus was dining in the home of a Pharisee, a woman of the city who was a sinner came and stood at his feet weeping. Standing there while Jesus reclined at the table, she wet his feet with her tears, wiped them with the hair of her head, and anointed him with a precious perfume. Simon the Pharisee, who had been a witness to the proceedings, was indignant that Jesus had permitted a sinner to touch him in such an intimate way. Jesus, recognizing Simon's indignation, responded to it by telling a story.

He told Simon that a certain creditor had two debtors; one owed him a great deal of money, and the other owed a lesser sum. When they could not pay, Jesus said, the creditor forgave both of the debtors. Now which of them will love him the most, Jesus asked. Simon rightly responded, "The one I suppose to whom he forgave more." Jesus assured Simon that he had judged rightly. Then he explained the source of Simon's feelings. He declared that Simon had not shown him the simple courtesies accorded someone in an Eastern home, such as providing water for the washing of his feet or according him the kiss of greeting, but the woman whose sins were many had washed his feet with her tears and dried them with her hair. She loved much because she knew the sins that had been forgiven were many. Simon did not have much love to give because there was no sense of sin and its forgiveness in his life.

When gratitude goes, it takes everything else with it. Pete Rose, a professional baseball player in his mid-forties, still plays the game as though he were only a boy. Someone asked Pete Rose whether or not the legs are the first thing that goes in professional baseball. Pete responded by declaring that it was not the legs, but rather the inner desire is the first to go. When the inner desire goes, the legs and everything else follows. The gratitude that floods our souls from having been touched by the living, saving love of Jesus Christ is an inner dynamic which, if missing, takes all our powers to serve with it. A sense of the meeting in which God's grace, demonstrated through Christ's love, proved capable of forgiving our worst and calling forth our best, must be kept alive as long as we live.

At our best, the church has always insisted on the primacy of Christian experience, the "being with

Jesus" that caused the council and the entire city to stand in awe of Peter and John and the other disciples (Acts 4:13 RSV). That experience, which cannot be inherited, must be ours and not just in a historical sense, but in an existential way.

Moses made it clear to the people of Israel during their trek to the Promised Land that it was not enough that some generation before them had stood on the side of the holy mountain, had spoken face to face with the living God. Moses made it clear that they could not be the people of God unless their own souls were scorched with the holy fire, until they stood face to face with the living God (Deut. 5:1 RSV).

Until that meeting becomes a reality and unless it is kept vitally alive in our memory and experience, motivating someone to serve and to lay down one's life for others is like pushing a wagon up a hill with a rope. When, through the historic spiritual disciplines, we become responsive to our own spiritual needs and become sensitized to the ever-present realization of the sins from which Christ has saved us and continues to save us, we become like that well-known lay pastor who said that he gave his soul, his body, and his possessions and grieved because there was no more to give. Like the woman in Bethany, who started to portion out her precious jar of ointment, but found it impossible to withhold even a part of it, we are continually overwhelmed by the realization of his saving, redeeming love, and with a lump in our throats, we lay down our lives for his sake and for the sake of the world.

We draw strength from our life-changing encounter with the Savior, whether the experience was sudden or gradual, and the continuation of his saving acts fills us more completely with awe and wonder regarding his love. Not only do we have the strength that comes from knowing that God is love and that we have ourselves experienced him, and continue to experience him as a pardoning God, but we have the additional incentive that comes from knowing that he sent us to share his love with the rest of his creation.

Paul has described that experience which is often referred to as the "poorest of trades but the noblest of callings" as having been "called to be an apostle, set apart for the Gospel of God" (Rom. 1:1 RSV). We may have experienced the call of God on our lives as an inner compulsion of the kind which Amos described when he said, "The Lord took me from following the flock" (Amos 7:15 RSV). Whether we were brought to that moment suddenly and dramatically or whether it gradually overtook us, we have all faced God's question to Isaiah, "Whom shall I send and who will go for us?" (Isa. 6:8 RSV). Our summons to service may have been as simple, and yet profound, as the quiet invitation to the fisherman of Galilee which Jesus issued when he said, "Follow me" (Mark 1:17 RSV). In whatever form and way the call came, we recognized it as a divine imperative. Like the experience of grace that took away our sin and made us new creatures, this call to service must be kept alive within our souls.

With the call comes a sense of destiny which nothing can replace. The call makes us a herald—saves us from being a hired hand. We are not like so many peddlers of the faith. We have drunk deeply of the fountain of God's love and have been set apart by

our call and the recognition of it by the church
through our ordination to proclaim the unsearchable
riches of Jesus Christ to the entire earth. Our chief
desire can never be career advancement, but must
always be a desire for subjectivity to the leading of
God's spirit. Shaped and molded by the seminary, we
nonetheless know that beneath and beyond all other
credentials is the profound realization that the
Almighty has placed his hand on us and has set us
apart for ministry.

A strong conviction about our call will bring with it
the belief that if we will cooperate, God will engineer
our circumstances. In the words of Wesley's
Watchnight Service, "Put me to what thou wilt . . .
put me to doing. . . ." Once that conviction is
captured, we are saved from "bad" appointments
and from the belief that somehow our careers have
gotten bogged down. The Christ, who without
apology sent his disciples out as lambs into the midst
of ravenous wolves, need not apologize to us for
using us in whatever way and in whatever place he
needs.

None of us is so naive as to maintain that our
appointment-making system has achieved perfection. Nor are our motives, or those of our leaders,
crystal clear. It is too late for us to talk about
innocence. We can, however, be saved from our
negative thoughts about the imperfections of the
system by a renewed conviction that God is bigger
than all of it. When we know that God has asked us to
serve, it can make all the difference in the quality of
our service.

If we are like the candidate who once said to
Bishop Arthur Moore that he was thinking about

taking up the ministry, then perhaps we should heed the advice of the bishop when he said to that candidate, "You should just put it down." William James was right when he declared that religion is either like a dull habit or an acute fever. Those who keep the fires burning brightly are ones who are steadily sure that they have been asked by the Lord of life to lay down their lives for him.

Several months ago an individual requested membership in our church. An older man, he seemed to be driven by an inordinate desire to become quickly active in our fellowship. In discussing his commitment I asked him why he had chosen to make that commitment. He responded by saying that left to himself he had long since given up on the church and was frankly disgusted with it. He has a grandson, however, and his grandson had asked him to join him in a commitment to Christ and to the church.

When I asked him about the grandson, I learned that the young man had just completed a degree in engineering at a fine university and had elected upon graduation to answer God's call to preach and was attending seminary. Then, almost as in a postscript, he said, "My grandson is blind." A brave young man who adores his grandfather had asked him to give his life to the same God to whom he was giving his. The request was larger than any misgivings on the part of the grandfather because it came from his grandson.

We are not ministers purely by choice. We were also chosen. Watchman Nee was right when he declared that to have God do his work through us is better than a lifetime of human striving. God does, of

course, work through all persons who have the
spiritual eyesight to see the vast needs about us. We
have the motivation, however, that comes from
knowing that we have been set apart for representative service, to be a sign to the church and to the
world. God has called us to make our lives and our
ministries sacramental—to live and serve so as to
make visible, put into time and space, the redeeming
activity of God in Jesus Christ. To be captured and
held by that high calling is to be motivated beyond
measure.

Our conversion, our call to serve, and the
continuing realization that the demons from which
Christ saved us were not banished altogether, but
still wait in the wings eager to step back onto the
stage . . . all of these are kept vividly alive within us
through a regular disciplined life of prayer. By
prayer I do not mean what one man shared with
me, saying, "When I am having a good day I send
up little happy thoughts to God." I am speaking of a
systematic discipline that is as regular as the intake
of food.

Several years ago I enjoyed taking a Wesleyan
heritage tour throughout England. I viewed with
great interest the church in Bristol with its vantage
point from which Wesley could observe his preachers in action. I think perhaps that was the forerunner
to our video practice preaching classes. I saw
Wesley's study desk and saw that the footrest on
which he placed his feet during the long hours he
spent reading and studying was almost worn
through. I thought of the fertility of his mind, the
vastness of his intellect, as I saw displays of his
creativity in the parsonage in London.

When I went to his upstairs bedroom, however, I felt closest to the heartbeat of the Wesleyan revival when I knelt for a moment on the little prayer stool on which Wesley began every day. Reading and studying is, of course, important, and we must read widely and continually. Bishop Asbury, however, captured the mind of Wesley and I believe of our Christ, when he said that the devil doesn't care how much you read as long as you don't pray. A pastor too busy, too undisciplined, to make a regular place for prayer is going out into the fields white unto harvest with a sword that has no edge.

During the bitterly cold month of February in 1984, my wife and I entertained some out-of-town guests in our guest house at the parsonage. Conveniently situated just behind the main house, the guest rooms are located above the garage and my at-home study. They come complete with their own hot water heater, air conditioning, and heating. My wife and I noticed on the third morning of our guests' stay with us, however, that they did not appear refreshed or rested after their night in the guest house. As I observed their less-than-cheerful manner at the breakfast table, the horrible thought occurred to me that perhaps I had forgotten to turn on the hot water heater which supplies the guest house. Tentatively, I asked them whether or not there had been any hot water, whereupon they almost exploded, with their "No! We have not had any hot water for the three days we have been here."

Following their outburst, I asked them, "Why didn't you say something?"

They said, "We thought you had run out of hot water."

I left the room shaking my head, leaving it to my wife to explain why they had not had any hot water for showers. All that time they had been thinking we had run out of hot water, but the truth was that the hot water had never been turned on.

Sometimes we sound as though God has run out of resources and power to revive our church and to save this world. The problem is not, however, that God has run out of power, the problem is we have not been turned on to that power. We cannot receive the empowerment that comes from God unless we are open enough to receive the gift of power.

The early church was shaken and empowered by the Holy Spirit while they were praying. The gift of the Holy Spirit was not given to them as a once-and-for-all gift, but was offered as a continuing gift as they continued to be open to receive him. Although Peter and John and the others were without vast lands, buildings, and reserves, they nonetheless had the power to say to crippled persons, "Stand up and walk." Indeed, they worked innumerable miracles on their way to and from the place of prayer. They were always praying. The place in which they prayed was not shaken once by God's spirit, but again and again. Each time God wanted to send them on an errand, he had to interrupt their prayers. Having a time and a place to pray was to them more basic than bread. This "towardness" toward God made it possible for him to let his power flow through them into the world.

Once while traveling in Macedonia, I saw a large flock of storks. Never having seen the large birds before, I was eager to learn all about them. I discovered that although they nested in Macedonia, they were migratory birds who wintered elsewhere. In the fall of that same year I was touring in Northern Israel and saw some storks circling over the mountains of the Golan Heights. I asked our guide, who was something of a naturalist, about those storks, telling him that I had seen some in Northern Greece. He explained that since the seasons had changed, the storks were on their way south to the continent of Africa, where they would spend the winter. Seeing that the storks were only lazily gliding about the mountains, I asked our guide why the storks didn't set out on their journey. He explained that their bodies were too heavy and their wings too weak to make the journey under adverse circumstances. They were waiting there in the mountainous area until they found a favorable wind current. Once they had a favorable wind under their wings, they would then begin the journey to their winter home.

We are discovering in these difficult days that our power is not sufficient to save and redeem the world. We cannot, in fact, maintain a capacity to serve or to make ourselves available to others unless the dynamic of God's Holy Spirit is powerfully operative within us. The spirit alone, "Christ within us," is our only hope for the manifestation of God's glory in our time.

Prayer is not productive of some kind of magical power. Prayer for us is like the rudder on the end of the windmill. Systematic prayer keeps us open to the power that comes from God through the spirit who wills to dwell within us. The spirit brings with him the gifts necessary for building up the community of faith. We cannot settle for Simon Peter as he was before Pentecost, nor can we serve effectively within our own strength. To attempt it will produce a plethora of books and articles on ministerial burnout and will lead to innumerable seminars on how ministers can save themselves.

Not along after my arrival in Houston, Texas, a friend took me out in his helicopter to visit a drilling rig in the Gulf of Mexico. I was fascinated to find, seventy-five miles out from Galveston, a rig with all the comforts of our modern-day society. There was a stainless steel kitchen complete with an ice cream parlor, there were color T.V. sets, telephones—an unbelievable set-up to give the workers all the comforts of home.

My friend's explanation concerning the scientific data that had prompted him and his company to invest more than $75 million for the right to drill there was pretty much lost on me. The material was too esoteric, too technical for me to comprehend. During our tour of the facility, however, I saw one worker whose job appeared to be extremely simple. He was dropping some kind of blunt piece of metal with a rag tied around it first through one pipe and then through the other. I asked my friend to explain the meaning of that procedure. He chuckled and explained that that little instrument was called a "rabbit." He said that oil men have long since learned that all the millions you invest to drill and to purchase equipment are for nothing if you lower one pipe that is clogged into the earth. Oil will not flow through a clogged pipe.

We are learning slowly and painfully in our denomination, The United Methodist Church, that structure alone will not save us. If the proliferation of bureaucracy and the investment of millions could have renewed the church, we would have long since experienced a genuine renewal. Is the path we should take too simple to be followed?

"You shall receive power," Jesus said, "when the Holy Spirit has come upon you; and you shall be my witnesses . . ." (Acts 1:8 RSV). Power is available. Our prayers and the prayers of our people can unclog the channels through which the riches of God's grace can reach out to the whole earth.